The
Vegetarian Touch

The Vegetarian Touch

Introduced by Gail Duff

WINDWARD

Editor: Julia Canning
Art editor: Mike Rose
Production: Richard Churchill

Published by Windward, an imprint
owned by W.H.Smith & Son Limited
Registered No. 237811 England
Trading as WHS Distributors,
St. John's House, East Street,
Leicester LE1 6NE

© Marshall Cavendish Limited 1985

ISBN 0-7112-0417-9

Printed and bound in Hong Kong by
Dai Nippon Printing Company

Contents

Introduction

Vegetarian food has become delicious and exciting – no longer is it 'food fit for cranks and extremists'. In fact many households, whether they are accustomed to eating meals without meat or not, are now turning towards vegetarian-style menus with enthusiasm.

The ingredients that make up vegetarian meals are combinations of the old favourites, such as cheese and eggs, together with newly accepted foods, such as chick-peas, millet and exotic vegetables. The mixture has enabled us to experiment with new tastes and textures and has led us to be far less conservative in our cooking and eating habits. A new breed of cooks, both professional and in the home, has for the past few years been developing new recipes and experimenting with new cooking methods to produce a real vegetarian cuisine. No one who likes good food, whether they are vegetarian or not, could fail to enjoy the dishes and ideas in the following pages.

The main reason why many people are becoming vegetarian at the moment is one of health. A vegetarian diet contains fewer animal fats than a meat diet and very often includes more whole grain products and fresh fruits and vegetables, all of which provide fibre as well as other nutrients.

Another good reason for including vegetarian meals in your weekly diet, is the fact that they are very economical. You are not buying expensive protein foods, such as meat or fish, but relying more on vegetables, pulses and small amounts of cheese or nuts. This will help the family budget and also allow you to splash out on extra special ingredients when you are entertaining.

The recipes in this book are suitable for vegetarians and non-vegetarians alike. If you are a vegetarian family, the recipes will go a long way to ensuring that you are eating the widest possible range of delicious and nutritious foods. If you are going to continue to eat meat, but wish to include more meat-free recipes in your menu plan for the week, they will help to add variety to your diet. If you have one vegetarian in the family or are having vegetarian friends for a meal, they can be an absolute life-saver.

The same rules for menu planning apply to vegetarian dishes as they do to mixed diet dishes. Simply make them as varied as possible. An extreme example of a badly planned menu is a cheese dip for a first course, a cheese based main course and cheesecake for dessert. Instead, start with a soup or something nutty, such as Spinach nut pasties (page 42). Follow this with a cheese based dish such as Cheese and chive soufflé or Swiss cheese fondue (both on page 61), finish with Spiced pears (page 98) or Redcurrant sorbet (page 102).

If your main meal is based on pulses, a cheesy first course, such as Melted Mozzarella sandwiches (page 39) or Tomatoes with cheese filling (page 33), would be quite appropriate.

Besides being more appealing to the palate, well balanced meals will provide a wide range of nutrients – an important factor in a vegetarian diet.

Planning Menus

The recipes are grouped under practical chapter headings so that they can be easily selected to create menus both for family meals and entertaining.

Vegetarian Ingredients

Cheese

Cheese is an excellent source of protein, vitamins A and D and also of vitamin B12, which is lacking in plant protein foods such as nuts and pulses. Basically, there are two types of cheese available, hard cheese and soft cheese.

Hard cheeses include the types such as Cheddar, Cheshire, Edam, Gouda, Gruyère, Emmenthal and Parmesan. Most have a high fat content. Cheddar and Gruyère for example, have around 34g per 100g and Edam and Gouda 22g and 26g respectively.

The problem for most strict vegetarians up until recently has been that hard cheeses are made by adding the animal product, rennet, to the milk in order to curdle it. Now, however, rennet-free cheeses are available from most health shops. These are made in such varieties as Cheddar and Cheshire. If you enjoy Italian cookery, an excellent substitute for Parmesan is a small, hard Swiss cheese, often made in a pyramid shape, called Geska.

The rules for buying and storing vegetarian cheeses are the same as for conventionally made hard cheeses. They may well be vacuum packed, in which case keep them in the refrigerator, still in the pack, until about an hour before needed. Open the pack and leave the cheese to breathe for a while at room temperature. Once opened, wrap the cheese in cling film or foil and store it again in the refrigerator.

If you find vegetarian cheeses too mild for your taste, store them, still in their pack, for up to two weeks in the refrigerator – this will mature their flavour.

Soft cheeses, such as cream, curd and cottage cheeses, fromage blanc and Quark are made without rennet and are therefore suitable for strict vegetarians. Cream cheese has a high fat content; ideally it should be kept for special occasions or mixed with other types. Curd cheese is a medium-fat cheese with a stiff texture and tangy but creamy flavour. Cottage cheese, with its soft, lumpy texture, is the lowest in fats. It has a pleasant bland flavour, which mixes well with both sweet and savoury ingredients.

Quark is a low-fat cheese, made by introducing a yoghurt-type culture to the milk which gives it a light, fresh flavour. Fromage blanc has a rich, creamy flavour but a thin texture; it is a low- to medium-fat cheese.

All soft cheeses should be stored in the refrigerator and ideally eaten within three days of purchase. Use them for dips, spreads, pâtés and salads. Beat them with eggs to make quiche fillings or with sweet ingredients to make cheesecakes.

Yoghurt

Yoghurt makes a useful between meals snack. It can be spooned over cereals or fresh, dried or cooked fruits and used in both sweet and savoury dishes.

Yoghurt contains vitamins A and D, some B vitamins, calcium and small amounts of protein. If eaten regularly, it will help the body to manufacture its own B vitamins. It can also reduce excess acid in the stomach and can, again if eaten frequently, help to reduce hay fever.

There are many different types of yoghurt on the market. The fruit-flavoured ones contain added white sugar and very often colouring and preservative. If health is your concern, it is better to buy natural yoghurt and flavour it yourself.

Natural yoghurts can be made from skimmed or whole milk, so choose the one which suits you best. Whole milk varieties contain more fat. Some varieties have extra vitamins A and D added; others have been made by adding sugar to the milk. Those to be found in health food shops are very often made from whole milk and yoghurt culture alone. Goat's milk and sheep's milk varieties are also available.

Milk

Milk should be regarded more as a nutritious food than as a drink, since it contains a wide range of nutrients. Vitamins A, D and some B vitamins are present, plus calcium and a small amount of protein.

Raw milk has not been pasteurised, thus more nutrients are preserved.

Whole pasteurised milk is the milk that has been heated to around 72C/16F to destroy bacteria. Some nutrients are also destroyed.

Gold top milk comes from Channel Island and Devon cattle and has a higher fat and nutrient content.

Homogenised milk has been heat treated to break up the fat globules and distribute them throughout the milk. There is therefore no 'top-of-the-milk'. Homogenised milk can be frozen.

Sterilized milk has undergone a greater degree of heat treatment, therefore destroying even more nutrients. It will keep fresh for a week without refrigeration, but has a slight caramel flavour.

Ultra heat treated (UHT) milk has been homogenised and further heat treated to give it an unrefrigerated shelf life of six months. Its vitamin C content is considerably reduced and the flavour altered.

Skimmed milk is pasteurised milk that has had virtually all its fat content removed. It is lower in vitamins A and D than whole milk. Semi-skimmed milk has had half the fat content removed, while skimmed milk powder is produced by spray-drying skimmed milk.

Goat's milk Goat's milk is becoming increasingly popular as it has been found that both children and adults who are allergic to cow's milk can drink goat's milk without problems. Goat's milk has a higher mineral content than cow's milk, slightly more vitamin A and twice the vitamin D. It has slightly more fat but this is distributed throughout the milk, making it more easily digestible. Goat's milk can be bought from many health shops and larger supermarkets.

Both untreated and pasteurised milk will keep in a refrigerator for up to three days or in a cool larder for up to two.

Eggs

Eggs are another high protein food, providing an excellent source of vitamin B12. They also contain other B vitamins, vitamins A and D, small amounts of vitamin E and iron, calcium, potassium and magnesium. They are digested very slowly and therefore make meals that will keep you satisfied for a long time. Easy to eat and highly nutritious, they make an ideal food for all the family, from babies of eight months to grandparents.

Eggs are one of the most versatile foods in anyone's kitchen. They can be served at any time of the day and in both sweet and savoury dishes. Try them boiled, scrambled or fried for snack meals, or turn them into omelettes, soufflés, soufflé omelettes or roulades.

Vegetables

Needless to say, vegetables play a large part in a vegetarian diet. In fact there are so many interesting varieties, supplying such a wide range of goodness, that they should be an important part in the daily menus of everyone. Turn them into soups or delectable first courses. Make a crunchy vegetable salad as a light meal, or serve hot vegetables as an accompaniment to a main meal. You can even make a main dish with a vegetable base. See Bulgarian vegetable stew (page 45).

Much of our vitamin C comes from vegetables, mainly from the green, leafy types but also, surprisingly, from ingredients like potatoes and cauliflower. Carrots, other red coloured vegetables and some of the darker green leaves provide vitamin A. The root vegetables, asparagus and beans provide B vitamins, while vitamin K is found in significant amounts in green vegetables.

Most vegetables are a good source of potassium and also supply plenty of fibre.

When buying vegetables always make sure that they look fresh. At home, keep them in a cool, dark place. Leafy greens and salad vegetables are best stored in a plastic bag in the bottom of the refrigerator. Mushrooms will keep well in a paper bag inside a polythene one. Leave root vegetables and onions unwashed or peeled, and store in a cool larder.

Fresh fruit

Fresh fruit can make a sweet, juicy snack at any time of the day. Serve it chopped into muesli or other cereals at breakfast; eat it with cheese for lunch; add it to vegetable soups and some savoury dishes (see Curried apple soup page 14); and use it for all kinds of desserts from a fresh fruit salad to a Hazelnut and raspberry meringue (page 103).

Fresh fruits are an excellent source of dietary fibre, most contain good supplies of vitamin C. Some fruits will also provide vitamin A.

Always make sure that fruit really is fresh when you buy it. Store apples, pears and citrus fruits in a cool, dark place for up to one week. Soft fruits are best eaten on the day of purchase, but will keep in a cool place for up to a day. Refrigerating them tends to harm their flavour. Stone fruits

will keep in the refrigerator for up to two days, grapes and kiwi fruits for up to four days.

Dried fruit

In a healthy diet, dried fruits are excellent to use as alternative sweeteners. Stew cooking apples with chopped dates, for example, and there is no need to add sugar. Mueslis and other breakfast cereals can also be sweetened entirely with dried fruits. The traditional use for dried fruits is in baking. See such recipes as Dundee cake and Apricot spice cake (both on page 110).

There is no vitamin C in dried fruits, but most are good sources of vitamin B1 and peaches and apricots of vitamin A. The mineral content is high and all are excellent sources of dietary fibre.

If you buy dried fruits from the supermarket you will notice that they look very shiny and do not stick together. This is because they have been coated with a mineral oil. Wash this off the fruits before using – put the fruits in a colander and rinse them with cold water. The varieties that you can usually buy in wholefood shops have no coating and therefore look duller and stickier.

Dried fruits keep well in airtight containers for up to one month. After this they may start to dry or form a sugary coating – they can still be used for cooking but are not so good raw.

Pulses

The term pulses covers the many varieties of dried beans, peas and lentils. These are invaluable in a vegetarian diet since they are excellent sources of protein, some B

vitamins and iron. They must however be eaten with a grain product in order to supply your body with the right sort of protein. Beans on toast is the obvious example, but see also Moors and christians (page 57) and Soya burgers (page 54). The chick-pea dip known as Hummus (page 26), eaten with pitta bread, is another perfect combination.

Pulses are now widely available in supermarkets and health food shops. Store them in airtight containers for up to 6 months. After this their skins may toughen causing the cooking time to be longer.

The method of cooking all the types of pulse is the same except for the timing. Recent research has shown that some types, in particular red, black, brown and white kidney beans, flageolets and pinto, haricot and aduki beans, may cause stomach upsets if they have not been boiled rapidly for at least 10 minutes, so incorporate this into your soaking and cooking method.

Beans can either be soaked overnight or quick-soaked on the same day. To soak overnight, simply leave them, covered with cold water, in a saucepan. When you are ready to cook them, first bring them to the boil, boil for 10 minutes and then drain. Cook them finally in fresh water. To quick-soak beans, put them into a saucepan and cover with cold water. Bring them to the boil and boil for 10 minutes. Remove the pan from the heat and leave

the beans to soak for 2 hours. Drain and cook with fresh water.

Cooking times:
Mung beans, aduki beans: 45 – 60 minutes
Black-eyed peas: 1 hour
Kidney beans, haricot beans, flageolets: 1½ – 2 hours
Butter beans: 2 hours
Chick-peas: up to 3 hours
Soya beans: 4 hours

Whole lentils can be soaked in cold water for 1-2 hours before cooking. This speeds up the cooking time slightly but is not absolutely essential. They become soft in 45 minutes to 1 hour. Split red lentils and split yellow and green peas need no soaking. They are usually used for making soups or purées and will soften in 45 minutes.

Once pulses have been cooked, they become an extremely versatile ingredient in the vegetarian kitchen. They might seem a little bland when served completely plainly, but add a tasty dressing and some chopped raw vegetables and they become an appetizing and colourful salad. See Two-bean salad (page 72). Add spicy vegetable sauces and you have delicious main meals. Spoon them on top of rice, layer them in a lasagne, put them into pasties and pies or purée them to make dips, pâtés and croquettes.

Pulses need not be completely cooked

before adding them to other dishes. They can actually be cooked with stock, vegetables and flavouring ingredients to make casseroles and soups. See Bean and vegetable soup (page 16) and Lentil and lemon soup (page 19).

The soya bean

The soya bean is so versatile that it deserves a special mention. It is high in protein and B vitamins, and has a delicious glossy texture when cooked. There are many soya bean products which are extremely useful in vegetarian cookery.

Soy sauce This is used widely in China and Japan and will add a salty flavour to soups, casseroles, salad dressings and stir-fried dishes.

Miso This is a thick, dark brown paste made from fermented soya beans. It is used in soups and vegetable casseroles to add protein, B vitamins and flavour.

Tofu This is also known as soy bean curd and is like a soya bean cheese. It comes in soft white blocks and has until now only been used in Eastern dishes. However, wholefood and vegetarian cooks have found that it is good in sauces, salad dressings and cheesecakes.

Soya flour This is a high protein flour made from finely ground soya beans. Small amounts can be added to baked goods and it can be used for sauces.

Soya milk This is a substitute milk made from soya beans. It looks and tastes very much like the real thing and can be used in the same way. It is ideal for those allergic to cow's milk.

Nuts and seeds

Nuts and seeds will also provide protein in a vegetarian diet but, like pulses, they must be combined with a grain product in order to supply the right type of protein for good health. The children's favourite peanut butter on wholewheat bread is a simple example. See also Nutty brown rice (page 56).

Nuts and seeds are also rich in minerals and contain, in varying quantities, B vitamins, and vitamins C, D and E. Never buy more than one month's suppy of nuts or seeds at a time and store them in airtight containers.

Nuts are extremely versatile. Add them to muesli or cereals for breakfast, or nibble them with dried fruit as a snack. They also make nutritious main meals, such as Carrot and nut roast (page 55), or delicious desserts, like Date and walnut apples (page 98).

Of the seeds, sesame seeds feature strongly in vegetarian cookery, tahini, a paste made from ground sesame seeds, is handy for dips and dressings.

Cereals

There are many ingredients that come under the general heading of cereals, all of which add variety and goodness to the vegetarian diet. Both refined and unrefined cereals can be used, but the unrefined whole grains are the healthiest, providing more B vitamins, iron and calcium and a great deal more fibre. They are important in a vegetarian diet as they must be combined with pulses, nuts and seeds to make high protein meals.

Wheat Wholewheat grains can be cooked whole and served as an accompaniment to a main meal.

Cracked wheat can be soaked and used as a salad, but most often it is sprinkled over breads.

Bulgur (burghul) wheat has been pre-cooked and cracked. Before serving, it need only be soaked for a time in cold water. Use it for salads such as Bulgur wheat and parsley salad (page 68). It can also be used in casseroles.

The main use of wheat in the Western World is to grind it to make flour. Wholewheat flour is produced by simply grinding the grains, taking nothing away and adding nothing so that all the goodness and fibre are left.

An 81-85% extraction flour (sometimes called brown or wheatmeal) has had some of the outercoating or bran removed, but the germ which contains most of the vitamins and minerals still remains.

White flour is a 70% extraction, meaning that all the bran and most of the germ have been removed, leaving a product which has lost much of its goodness. Some B vitamins and calcium are added back artificially.

Unbleached white flour is a 70% extraction flour which has not undergone a chemical bleaching process, leaving it creamy coloured.

Strong flour is produced from what is known as hard wheat. It has a high gluten content and is recommended for bread making.

Granary bread meal is an 85% extraction flour which contains added gluten and malted grains of wheat and rye.

Wheat germ is the tiny nutritious part of the wheat grain. It is high in B vitamins, iron and vitamin E and can be sprinkled over cereals and chopped fruit or added to bread mixes.

Wheat bran is the outer coating of the wheat grain and is high in fibre. Sprinkle it over cereals or use it as a coating for croquettes.

Semolina is hard wheat which has been coarsely ground. Both refined and wholewheat varieties are available. Use it for milk puddings.

Pasta is also made from a hard wheat flour. Both white and wholewheat varieties are available in a wide variety of shapes and sizes. Spinach pasta can also be bought in the form of tagliatelle or lasagne. Fresh pasta is available from delicatessens which specialize in Italian food. Pasta makes a wide range of substantial main meals. See Creamy rigatoni (page 65) and Lentil lasagne (page 64).

Oats Oats can be bought in the form of whole oat grains (sometimes called groats) which can be cooked in a similar way to rice; coarse oatmeal which is normally used for porridge; and medium and fine oatmeal which are used for baking. Rolled oats are used mainly for muesli and also make delicious flapjacks and crumble toppings. Porridge oats have been steamed so that they cook quickly to make a creamy breakfast.

Barley Pearl barley and whole barley grains are used to enrich soups and casseroles (see Leek and barley soup page 18). Barley flakes are similar to rolled oats and are sometimes added to muesli; while barley flour can be used to make light pastries.

Rye Rye is most often sold in the form of flour, which is used with whole wheat flour to make rye bread.

Rice Both white and brown rice can be used in vegetarian cookery, but brown rice is the most nutritious since, like wholewheat, it still has its outer coating of bran. It also contains more iron, calcium, protein and B vitamins than the white varieties. Both long and short grain varieties of brown rice are available. The long grain is used mainly in savoury dishes, such as pilaffs, and is also cooked plainly to be served as an accompaniment. Short grain brown rice can be used for risottos as well as for rich milk puddings.

Brown rice takes longer to cook than white, 40-45 minutes as opposed to 15-20 minutes.

Buckwheat The tiny, heart-shaped grains of buckwheat are most often cooked to make a grain side dish known as Kasha. They have a distinct nutty flavour. Buckwheat flour can be made into pancakes and muffins. It is also made into a quick-cooking pasta.

Millet Takes the form of round, tiny yellow grains which, when cooked, make a fluffy, light textured side dish.

Sweeteners

A vegetarian diet need not be an austere one. You can still enjoy desserts and sweets. There are many different types of sweetener available, some are slightly healthier than others.

Sugar White sugar is made up only of sucrose which provides calories but no other nutrients. Demerara sugar contains small traces of minerals. Dark Barbados sugar contains small amounts of minerals and enough B vitamins to ensure its digestion without depleting your body's supplies. Molasses sugar, which is really dark and rich, is a better source of minerals and also contains B vitamins.

Molasses is high in minerals and B vitamins. It can be used in baking and is good for flavouring and sweetening cooked fruit.

Honey contains small amounts of vitamins A and C and those of the B group. The energy it gives is quickly available to the body and lasts longer than that obtained from white sugar. Honey has two thirds the calories of sugar, and is much sweeter, so that you need less.

Maple syrup is derived by boiling and reducing the sap of North American maple trees. It contains a high proportion of sugars but is also rich in minerals.

Malt extract is made from germinated barley grains. It is digested more slowly than sucrose so giving a constant supply of energy rather than a quick lift. It contains small amounts of protein, B vitamins and minerals.

Fats and oils

Butter can be used in vegetarian cookery, but many vegetarians prefer to use vegetable oils or a soft vegetable margarine, all of which are high in polyunsaturated fats and low in cholesterol.

When buying margarine, read the labels and choose one that is made only from vegetable ingredients. The softer a margarine, the more polyunsaturated fats it contains. Vegetable margarine can be spread on bread and used in baking. You can fry with it and toss it into cooked vegetables.

The best oils to buy are the named oils such as olive, sunflower, safflower, soya, groundnut, corn and sesame. Olive oil is the best for salads. Sunflower is a good universal oil, which can be used for both salads and for sautéeing. Groundnut oil is the one frequently chosen by the Chinese for stir-frying. Corn oil can be used for deep frying or for making cakes and pastries.

Savoury flavourings

Herbs and spices These feature frequently in vegetarian cooking and can turn plain ingredients into exotic dishes with flavours from all over the world.

Many recipes specify only the amount of fresh herbs. If you only have dried, use one third of the amount of fresh herbs given. Dried herbs are not suitable for uncooked recipes such as dips, but they can be added to salads if they are soaked in the dressing for 30 minutes before hand.

Many supermarkets now stock a wide range of fresh herbs. You can also try growing your own.

Store dried herbs in airtight containers and keep them for no longer than a year. Spices should also be bought in small amounts, kept in airtight containers and, like herbs, stored for no longer than a year, after which their flavour may deteriorate or alter.

Yeast extract A yeast extract, such as Marmite, will give extra flavour to savoury vegetarian dishes, particularly nut roasts, patties and vegetable casseroles.

Sweet flavourings

Vanilla and almond extracts Natural vanilla and almond extracts can be bought from delicatessens and health food shops. They have a finer flavour than those labelled 'flavouring'. Use them in desserts and in baking.

Carob Carob powder is a popular substitute for cocoa powder. It is produced from the carob bean and is high in vitamins and minerals. It is far sweeter than cocoa, so dishes made with it need less sugar. It also contains no caffeine.

Setting agents

Whether making savoury moulds or sweet jellies and mousses, some setting agent has to be used. Non-vegetarians can use gelatine, but as this is an animal product strict vegetarians prefer to use a substitute.

Agar-agar is a freeze-dried seaweed which comes in the form of small, off-white flakes. Two to three teaspoons should set 600ml/1 pint liquid. In order to achieve a set, boil the flakes in all or some of the cold liquid, acording to individual recipes.

Soups

**Soups add variety and interest to vegetarian meals –
start a meal in style with a smooth, chilled soup or warm
the family with a nourishing meal-in-a-bowl.**

Vegetable stock

MAKES ABOUT 2.3 L/4 PINTS

50 g/2 oz margarine
1 large onion, finely chopped
3 large carrots, chopped
3 celery stalks with leaves left on, roughly
  chopped
1 large turnip or parsnip, chopped
1 teaspoon light soft brown sugar
2.3 L/4 pints hot water
1 large bouquet garni, consisting of 8 parsley
  sprigs, 2 thyme sprays and 2 bay leaves,
  tied together
6 white peppercorns
1½ teaspoons salt
2 whole cloves

1 Melt the fat in a large saucepan
over moderate heat. Add the onion,
carrots, celery, turnip and sugar and
cook, stirring frequently, for 8-10
minutes until the onion is soft and
golden brown.
2 Pour in the hot water, then add the
bouquet garni, white peppercorns, salt
and cloves. Bring the liquid to the
boil, stirring frequently, then reduce
the heat and simmer, stirring occasionally, for 45 minutes.
3 Remove the pan from the heat and
pour the stock through a fine wire
strainer into a large mixing bowl.
Using the back of a wooden spoon,
press down on the vegetables to extract
all the juices. Discard the contents of
the strainer.
4 Set the strained vegetable stock
aside until completely cool. Transfer
the cold stock to a container, cover and
store in the refrigerator, or use as
required.

Summer pea soup

SERVES 4

1.5 kg/3 lb fresh peas in the pod
25 g/1 oz butter
½ Spanish onion, finely chopped
4 outer leaves cos lettuce, shredded
600 ml/1 pint hot vegetable stock
salt and freshly ground black pepper
150 g/5 oz natural yoghurt
½ teaspoon lemon juice (optional)

1 Shell the peas and weigh out 500
g/1 lb. Reserve 3-4 of the best empty
pods.
2 Melt the butter in a large, heavy-
based saucepan over low heat. Add the
onion, lettuce and the reserved pea
pods, cover the pan and cook the
vegetables gently for 10 minutes, stirring occasionally.
3 Add the peas to the pan, pour in
the hot stock and season to taste with
salt and pepper. Bring slowly to the
boil, cover, reduce heat and simmer
until the peas are very tender.
4 Remove the pan from the heat,
discard the pods, and allow the soup to
cool slightly. Purée the soup in a
blender, a batch at a time. Reserve 4
teaspoons yoghurt and add the rest to
the final batch of purée and blend this
batch again.
5 Pour all the puréed soup into a
bowl and refrigerate for about 2 hours,
stirring occasionally.
6 Just before serving, taste and adjust the seasoning; sharpen the soup
with a few drops of lemon juice if
liked. Pour the soup into 4 individual
bowls and swirl 1 teaspoon natural
yoghurt into each. Serve at once.

Gazpacho

SERVES 4

500 g/1 lb tomatoes, skinned and chopped
½ cucumber, peeled and chopped
1 green pepper, deseeded and chopped
1 small onion, coarsely chopped
1 clove garlic, chopped
2 slices white bread, crusts removed,
  crumbled
1 teaspoon salt, or to taste
2 tablespoons red wine vinegar
1 L/1¾ pints iced water
5 tablespoons olive oil
To serve
bread cubes, fried until golden
chopped hard-boiled egg
finely chopped cucumber
finely chopped green pepper
finely diced onion

1 In a large bowl, combine the tomatoes, cucumber, green pepper, onion,
garlic, bread, salt and vinegar. Add
the water and mix thoroughly.
2 Purée the mixture in a food processor or blender until smooth. Return
the purée to the large bowl and whisk
in the olive oil in a thin, steady stream.
3 Cover the bowl with cling film and
refrigerate for about 2 hours until
thoroughly chilled.
4 When the soup is well chilled, stir
thoroughly and taste and adjust seasoning. Pour into 4 chilled individual
soup bowls and serve at once. Hand
the fried bread cubes, hard-boiled egg,
cucumber, green pepper and onion
separately.

Gazpacho, a classic Spanish soup

Chilled carrot and orange soup

SERVES 4

500 g/1 lb carrots, thinly sliced
1 tablespoon vegetable oil
1 onion, finely chopped
2 tablespoons medium-dry sherry
600 ml/1 pint vegetable stock
salt and freshly ground black pepper
grated zest of 1 orange
juice of 3 large oranges

To garnish

4 very thin orange slices, rinds removed
1 small carrot, thickly grated

1 Heat the oil in a saucepan, add the onion and fry gently for 5 minutes until soft and lightly coloured. Add the sherry, and bring to the boil.
2 Add the sliced carrots and stock to the pan and season to taste.
3 Bring to the boil, stirring, then lower the heat, cover and simmer gently for 45 minutes until the carrots are very tender. Leave to cool.
4 Pass the soup through a sieve or purée in a blender. Pour the soup into a bowl, cover and refrigerate for at least 2 hours or overnight.
5 Just before serving, stir the orange zest and juice into the soup, then taste and adjust seasoning. Pour into 4 chilled individual soup bowls, float 1 orange slice on top of each bowl and arrange a little grated carrot on top of the slices. Serve at once.

Chilled cucumber soup

SERVES 4

1 large unpeeled cucumber, finely grated
500 g/1 lb natural yoghurt
2 tablespoons wine vinegar
2 tablespoons chopped fresh mint
2 tablespoons seedless raisins
2 hard-boiled eggs, finely chopped
1 large clove garlic, crushed
1 teaspoon caster sugar
1 large crisp dessert apple, cored and chopped
150 ml/1/4 pint soured cream

Curried apple soup

SERVES 4

500 g/1 lb dessert apples
few drops of lemon juice
15 g/1/2 oz butter
1/2 Spanish onion, finely chopped
1 tablespoon mild curry powder
600 ml/1 pint hot vegetable stock
piece of cinnamon stick
150 ml/1/4 pint milk
5 tablespoons single cream
thin lemon slices and watercress sprigs, to
    garnish

1 Peel, core and chop the apples, placing them in a bowl of cold water mixed with the lemon juice, to prevent discoloration.
2 Melt the butter in a heavy-based saucepan. Thoroughly drain the apples and add them to the pan with the onion. Cover and cook gently, stirring occasionally, until the apples and onion are soft but not coloured.
3 Add the curry powder and cook over moderate heat, stirring, for 2-3 minutes. Pour in the hot stock and add the cinnamon stick. Bring to the boil, cover the pan, and simmer for 10 minutes. Remove cinnamon stick.
4 Purée the soup in a blender or pass through a sieve. Allow to cool, then stir in the milk and cream. Refrigerate, covered for 2 hours.
5 Stir the soup and pour into 4 individual bowls. Garnish with lemon and watercress and serve.

1 In a large bowl combine all the ingredients and stir well to mix them thoroughly.
2 Cover the bowl and refrigerate for at least 3 hours.
3 Pour the soup into a tureen or spoon straight into individual bowls and serve chilled.

Yoghurt and lemon soup

SERVES 6

600 g/1¼ lb natural yoghurt, chilled
600 ml/1 pint tomato juice, chilled
1 teaspoon tomato purée
½ small cucumber, peeled and finely diced
1 green pepper, deseeded and finely chopped
2 spring onions, thinly sliced
juice and grated zest of 1 large lemon
salt and freshly ground black pepper
large pinch of cayenne pepper
½ teaspoon sweet paprika
1 tablespoon snipped chives
thin lemon slices, to garnish

1 Tip the yoghurt into a large bowl and gradually beat in the tomato juice and purée until the mixture is smooth and well blended.
2 Stir in the cucumber, green pepper, spring onions, lemon juice and zest. Season to taste with salt and black pepper; stir in cayenne and paprika.
3 Cover and refrigerate until needed. Just before serving, stir in the snipped chives. Pour into individual bowls, garnish with lemon slices and serve.

Chilled fruit soup

SERVES 4

225 g/8 oz fresh or frozen redcurrants
225 g/8 oz fresh or frozen blackcurrants
225 g/8 oz fresh or frozen raspberries
850 ml/1½ pints water
25 g/1 oz tapioca or sago
5 cm/2 inch cinnamon stick
2 thinly pared strips lemon zest
225 g/8 oz sugar
6 tablespoons soured cream

Far left: Curried apple soup is an exotic combination of flavours
Above: Chilled carrot and orange soup makes a popular starter

1 To prepare fresh fruit: strip the currants from their stems by drawing a fork down each stem. Pick over the raspberries, and reserve 4 for the garnish.
2 Put the fruits in a large, heavy-based saucepan with the water, tapioca, cinnamon stick, lemon zest and sugar.
3 Set the pan over moderate heat and bring to the boil. Lower the heat and cook gently, uncovered, for 20 minutes.
4 Remove from the heat and discard the cinnamon stick and lemon zest. Pass the soup through a sieve. Cool, then refrigerate for 1½ hours.
5 Pour the chilled soup into 4 chilled individual bowls. Beat the soured cream until smooth, then swirl a portion over each serving. Top each swirl of soured cream with a raspberry and serve at once.

Bean and vegetable soup

SERVES 4

250 g/9 oz dried haricot beans, soaked
    overnight and drained

1 tablespoon vegetable oil

1 large onion, chopped

2 leeks, chopped

3 celery stalks, chopped

2 carrots, sliced

2 cloves garlic, crushed (optional)

700 ml/1¼ pints vegetable stock

225 g/8 oz can tomatoes

1 teaspoon dried oregano

salt and freshly ground black pepper

1 Cover the beans with fresh hot
water and boil for 10 minutes, then
cover with fresh water and simmer for
about 2 hours until they are tender.
Drain well.

2 Heat the oil in a large saucepan,
add onion and fry for 2 minutes. Add
the leeks, celery and carrots to pan
with garlic, if using, and cook a
further 2 minutes.

3 Add the stock and beans, together
with the tomatoes and their juice, the
oregano and plenty of salt and pepper.
Bring to the boil, then lower the heat,
cover and simmer for 30 minutes until
the vegetables are tender. Serve.

Leekie oat broth

SERVES 4

100 g/4 oz leeks, thinly sliced

600 ml/1 pint vegetable stock or water

100 g/4 oz carrots, finely chopped

½ teaspoon dried mixed herbs

salt and freshly ground black pepper

25 g/1 oz porridge oats

150 ml/¼ pint milk

2 tablespoons single cream or evaporated milk

*Above: Leekie oat broth, a thick hearty
soup for winter days*
*Far right: Chunky soya vegetable soup is
a meal in itself*

To serve

100 g/4 oz Edam cheese, cubed

1 Pour the stock into a saucepan and
bring to the boil. Add the leeks,
carrots, herbs and salt and pepper to
taste. Lower the heat, cover and simmer for 15 minutes or until the vegetables are tender.

2 Sprinkle the oats into the soup, stir
in the milk and cook gently, uncovered, for 5 minutes, stirring occasionally, until thick. Stir in the cream
and heat through: do not boil.

3 To serve: ladle into a warmed
tureen or individual soup bowls and
mix the cubes of Edam cheese into the
soup. Serve at once, before the cheese
has completely melted.

Finnish vegetable soup

SERVES 4-6

500 g/1 lb potatoes (preferably new), diced
3 medium carrots, diced
100 g/4 oz cauliflower florets
50 g/2 oz frozen peas
100 g/4 oz frozen sliced green beans
850 ml/1½ pints water
salt and freshly ground black pepper
25 g/1 oz margarine or butter
25 g/1 oz plain flour
1 large egg yolk
4 tablespoons double cream
¼ teaspoon sweet paprika

To serve

2 tablespoons finely chopped fresh parsley
50 g/2 oz strong Cheddar or Cheshire cheese,
    finely grated

1 Put the potatoes, carrots, cauliflower, peas, beans and water into a large saucepan. Season well with salt and pepper, bring to the boil and simmer uncovered for 10 minutes or until tender.
2 Remove the pan from the heat and strain the stock into a bowl. Reserve the cooked vegetables.
3 Melt the margarine gently in the rinsed-out pan and sprinkle in the flour. Stir over low heat for 1-2 minutes until straw-coloured. Remove from the heat and gradually stir in the stock. Return to the heat and simmer, stirring, until the stock is thick and smooth.
4 In a small bowl, whisk the egg yolk into the cream with the paprika. Gradually whisk 4 tablespoons of the hot thickened stock into the egg and cream, then slowly stir the mixture back into the remaining thickened stock in the pan. Return the reserved vegetables to the pan, taste and adjust seasoning and heat through. Do not boil or it may curdle. Add a little extra water if the soup appears to be getting too thick.
5 To serve: ladle into 4 warmed individual soup bowls and sprinkle each serving with chopped parsley. Serve at once with grated cheese handed separately.

Chunky soya vegetable soup

SERVES 4

100 g/4 oz soya beans, soaked in cold water
    overnight
1 tablespoon vegetable oil
1 large onion, sliced
2 leeks, thickly sliced
50 g/2 oz carrots, thickly sliced
2 celery stalks, thickly sliced
50 g/2 oz turnips, cut into cubes
850 ml/1½ pints vegetable stock or
    water
1 tablespoon lemon juice
2 tablespoons tomato purée
1-2 tablespoons dried mixed herbs
100 g/4 oz courgettes, thickly sliced
a few tender cabbage or spinach leaves, finely
    shredded or chopped
salt and freshly ground black pepper
2 teaspoons toasted sesame seeds, to garnish
    (optional)

1 Drain the soaked beans, then put into a saucepan and cover with fresh cold water. Bring to the boil and boil for 10 minutes, then lower the heat, cover and simmer for 1½ hours.
2 After the beans have been cooking for 1 hour 20 minutes, heat the oil in a separate large saucepan. Add the onion and fry gently for 5 minutes until soft but not coloured. Add the leeks, carrots, celery and turnips and cook, stirring, for a further 2 minutes.
3 Stir in the stock, lemon juice, tomato purée and herbs.
4 Drain the beans and add to the pan. Bring to the boil, then lower the heat slightly, cover the pan and simmer for 1 hour.
5 Add the courgettes and cabbage and continue to cook for a further 15 minutes or until the vegetables are tender. Season with salt and pepper.
6 Pour into warmed individual soup bowls and garnish with a sprinkling of sesame seeds, if liked. Serve at once.

Provençal vegetable soup

SERVES 4-6

1.7 L/3 pints water
1 teaspoon salt
bouquet garni
1 large potato, diced
1 large onion, chopped
1 celery stalk, finely sliced
2 carrots, sliced
250 g/9 oz French beans, sliced
250 g/9 oz runner beans, sliced
2 courgettes, thickly sliced
100 g/4 oz dried wholewheat pasta shells or
    macaroni

Pistou sauce

3-4 large cloves garlic, peeled
4 tablespoons chopped fresh basil leaves
salt and freshly ground black pepper
50 g/2 oz grated Parmesan cheese
2 tomatoes, skinned, seeded and coarsely
    chopped
4 tablespoons olive oil

1 Put the water in a large flameproof casserole, add the salt and bring to the boil. Add the bouquet garni, potato, onion, celery, and carrots. Bring back to the boil, then cover the pan and simmer for about 10 minutes until the vegetables are almost tender.

2 Add the beans, courgettes and pasta to the casserole and simmer, uncovered, for 10-15 minutes until tender.

3 Meanwhile, make the pistou: put the garlic in a mortar with the basil and salt and pepper to taste, then pound to a paste. Gradually work in the cheese, alternating with the tomatoes. Slowly work in the olive oil, a few drops at a time to start with, to make a thick sauce.

4 Remove and discard the bouquet garni from the soup. Blend 4 tablespoons of the hot soup into the sauce, then stir the mixture into the soup.

5 Taste and adjust the seasoning. Pour into warmed individual soup bowls and serve at once.

Leek and barley soup

SERVES 4

4 leeks, sliced
50 g/2 oz pearl barley
1 tablespoon vegetable oil
1 small onion, chopped
2 carrots, sliced
400 g/14 oz can tomatoes
600 ml/1 pint vegetable stock or water
1/2 teaspoon dried mixed herbs
1 bay leaf
salt and freshly ground black pepper
215 g/7 1/2 oz can butter beans, drained

Cheesy bread

4 round slices French bread, 2 cm/3/4 inch
    thick
40 g/1 1/2 oz butter, for frying
1 clove garlic, cut in half
100 g/4 oz Cheddar cheese, grated

1 Heat the oil in a large saucepan, add the onion, leeks and carrots and fry gently for 3-4 minutes.

2 Add the tomatoes with their juice, the stock and the barley, herbs and bay leaf. Season to taste with salt and pepper. Bring to the boil, stirring, then lower the heat, cover and simmer for 50 minutes. Stir occasionally during this time.

3 Meanwhile, make the cheesy bread: melt the butter in a frying-pan and when it sizzles add the slices of French bread. Fry over fairly high heat, turning once, until the bread is crisp and golden brown on both sides. Remove from the pan, drain on absorbent paper and leave to cool.

4 Rub each side of fried bread with the cut sides of the garlic. Press the grated cheese evenly on to the slices of bread, dividing it equally between them. Heat the grill to high.

5 Remove the bay leaf from the soup, stir in the drained beans and heat through. Taste and adjust seasoning if necessary.

6 Toast the cheese-topped slices of bread until the cheese starts to bubble.

7 Ladle the soup into 4 warmed individual soup bowls and top each one with a slice of cheesy bread. Serve at once.

Thick country soup

SERVES 4

1 tablespoon vegetable oil
15 g/¹/₂ oz butter
1 onion, chopped
225 g/8 oz carrots, sliced
100 g/4 oz packet soup mix, containing a
    mixture of lentils, yellow and green split
    peas, pearl barley and oatmeal
850 ml/1¹/₂ pints vegetable stock
1 leek, white part only, chopped
1 celery stalk, chopped
1 teaspoon dried thyme
1 bay leaf
salt and freshly ground black pepper
1 tablespoon chopped fresh parsley

1 In a saucepan, heat the oil and butter and gently cook the onion and carrots for 10 minutes.
2 Add the soup mix together with the vegetable stock, leek, celery and herbs. Bring to the boil, then lower the heat, cover and simmer for about 45 minutes Remove the bay leaf from the soup, if liked.
3 Season the soup to taste with salt and pepper and stir in the parsley.
4 Ladle the soup into a warmed soup tureen or 4 individual bowls and serve at once.

Lentil and lemon soup

SERVES 4

100 g/4 oz split red lentils
1 tablespoon vegetable oil
2 celery stalks, chopped
1 onion, finely chopped
1 L/1³/₄ pints boiling water
2 vegetable stock cubes
grated zest and juice of 1 lemon
¹/₄ teaspoon ground cumin (optional)
salt and freshly ground black pepper
1 red pepper, deseeded and thinly sliced into
    rings

To garnish
1 lemon, thinly sliced
snipped chives (optional)

1 Melt the vegetable oil in a saucepan, add the celery and onion, then cover and cook gently for 4 minutes.
2 Remove the pan from the heat, then stir in the lentils and water, with the stock cubes. Add the lemon zest and juice, and the cumin, if using. Season to taste with salt and pepper. Cover and simmer over very gentle heat for 30 minutes.
3 Add the sliced pepper to the pan, cover and cook for a further 30 minutes. Taste and adjust seasoning.
4 Pour the soup into warmed serving bowls, float the lemon slices on top, then sprinkle over the chives, if using. Serve at once.

Far left: Leek and barley soup has a scrumptious toast garnish
Below: Thick country soup makes a nourishing family supper dish

Left: Mixed vegetable borshch
Below right: Spinach and potato soup

pan and stir in the milk off the heat.
4 Heat the purée gently until simmering then remove from heat and stir in the grated cheese. Season to taste with salt and pepper.
5 Pour the soup into 4 warmed individual soup bowls and swirl 1 tablespoon cream into each. Place a quarter of the cheese on top of each serving and sprinkle over a little chopped parsley. Serve at once.

Creamy spinach and potato soup

SERVES 4

500 g/1 lb spinach, central ribs removed, or 300 g/10 oz packet frozen spinach
500 g/1 lb potatoes, cut into chunks
25 g/1 oz margarine or butter
1 onion, chopped
600 ml/1 pint vegetable stock
few sprigs of parsley
pinch of freshly grated nutmeg
150 ml/¼ pint milk
150 ml/¼ pint single cream
2 teaspoons lemon juice
salt and freshly ground black pepper

Cheese floats

4 slices French bread, cut diagonally into 2 cm/¾ inch thick slices
75 g/3 oz Cheddar cheese, thinly sliced

1 Melt the margarine in a saucepan, add the onion and fry over moderate heat for 3 minutes, stirring. Add the spinach, potatoes, vegetable stock, parsley and nutmeg.
2 Bring to the boil, then lower the heat, cover and simmer for about 20 minutes, until potatoes are tender.
3 Heat the grill to high
4 Allow the mixture to cool slightly, then work in batches in a blender. Return to the rinsed-out pan, then stir in the milk, cream and lemon juice. Season with salt and pepper. Reheat very gently without boiling.
5 Meanwhile, make the cheese floats: toast the slices of bread on one side, then lay the cheese slices on the untoasted sides and grill until the cheese has melted.
6 Pour the soup into 4 warmed individual bowls and top each with a cheese float. Serve at once.

Mixed vegetable borshch

SERVES 6

400 g/14 oz cooked beetroot, peeled
1 large onion
200 g/7 oz carrots
200 g/7 oz celery
1.2 L/2¼ pints vegetable stock
1 tablespoon light soft brown sugar
2 tablespoons red wine vinegar
1 clove garlic, crushed with a pinch of salt
freshly ground black pepper

To garnish

150 ml/¼ pint soured cream
250 g/9 oz potatoes, boiled and cut into 5 mm/¼ inch dice
2 tablespoons chopped fresh parsley

1 Cut all the vegetables into matchstick strips.
2 Bring the stock to the boil, add the vegetables, sugar, vinegar and garlic and season with the pepper. Cover and simmer for 20 minutes.
3 To serve, ladle the soup into warmed individual bowls. Top each with a portion of soured cream. Scatter the diced potatoes on top and sprinkle over a little chopped parsley. Serve at once.

Cauliflower cheese soup

SERVES 4

250 g/9 oz cauliflower, broken into small florets
50 g/2 oz margarine or butter
1 onion, chopped
1 potato, thinly sliced
300 ml/½ pint vegetable stock
300 ml/½ pint milk
50 g/2 oz Cheddar cheese, grated
salt and freshly ground black pepper

To garnish

4 tablespoons single cream
25 g/1 oz Cheddar cheese, grated
1 tablespoon chopped fresh parsley

1 Melt margarine in a large saucepan, add the onion and fry gently for 5 minutes until soft and lightly coloured. Add the cauliflower florets and potato slices. Cover and cook the vegetables for 10 minutes.
2 Stir in the stock, bring to the boil, then cover and simmer for about 25-30 minutes, until all the vegetables are soft. Allow to cool slightly.
3 Transfer the vegetables and stock to the goblet of a blender and work until smooth. Return the purée to the

Creamy mushroom soup

SERVES 4

250 g/9 oz button mushrooms

50 g/2 oz margarine or butter

2 tablespoons plain flour

600 ml/1 pint milk

75 g/3 oz full-fat soft cheese with chives

2 teaspoons lemon juice

salt and freshly ground black pepper

1 tablespoon snipped chives, to garnish

1 Finely chop the mushrooms, reserving 2-3 whole ones for the garnish. Melt half margarine in a frying-pan. Add the chopped mushrooms and fry gently for about 5 minutes until soft. Set aside.

2 Melt remaining margarine in a large saucepan, sprinkle in flour and stir over low heat for 1-2 minutes until it is straw-coloured. Remove from the heat and gradually stir in milk. Return to the heat and simmer, stirring, until the mixture is thick and smooth.

3 Remove from the heat, add the cheese a little at a time and stir until melted. Stir in the mushrooms, their juices and the lemon juice. Season to taste with salt and pepper. Return the pan to the heat and simmer for 2-3 minutes, stirring.

4 Pour into 4 warmed soup bowls. Float a few slices of mushrooms on top of each serving. Sprinkle lightly with chives and serve at once.

Green pepper cream soup

SERVES 4

250 g/9 oz green peppers, deseeded

25 g/1 oz margarine or butter

1 large onion, chopped

1 clove garlic, chopped

15 g/½ oz plain flour

600 ml/1 pint vegetable stock

1 teaspoon chopped fresh herbs or ½ teaspoon dried mixed herbs

salt and freshly ground black pepper

1 teaspoon lemon juice

150 ml/¼ pint single cream

1 Cut a few very thin rings from one of the peppers and set aside for garnish. Chop the remainder.

2 Melt the margarine in a heavy-based saucepan. Add the chopped peppers, onion and garlic and cook over very low heat for about 10 minutes, stirring frequently, until the vegetables are soft but not brown.

3 Sprinkle in the flour and cook for 1-2 minutes, stirring, then gradually stir in the stock. Add the herbs, and season to taste with salt and pepper. Cover the saucepan and cook gently for 20-25 minutes until the vegetables are tender.

4 Leave to cool slightly, then transfer to a blender and blend for about 5 seconds until smooth. If you do not have a blender, work the vegetables through a sieve while still hot. Return the soup to the rinsed-out pan, add lemon juice and cream, then taste and adjust seasoning if necessary. Heat through thoroughly, but take care not to boil.

5 Pour the soup into 4 warmed individual soup bowls. Garnish each serving with a pepper ring and serve the soup at once.

Tomato rice soup

SERVES 4

500 g/1 lb fresh tomatoes, chopped
400 g/14 oz can tomatoes
1 tablespoon tomato purée
150 ml/¼ pint water
salt and freshly ground black pepper
50 g/2 oz long-grain rice
2 tablespoons medium sherry
1 tablespoon finely chopped fresh parsley, to
　garnish

1　Put all the ingredients except the rice, sherry and parsley into a large saucepan. Bring to the boil, stirring, then lower the heat, cover and simmer for 30 minutes.
2　Pass the contents of the saucepan through a sieve, or leave to cool slightly, then purée in a blender and sieve.
3　Pour the sieved tomato purée back into the rinsed-out pan and bring back to the boil. Stir in the rice, lower the heat, cover and simmer for about 15 minutes or until the rice is tender.
4　Stir in the sherry, taste and adjust seasoning, then pour into warmed individual soup bowls. Sprinkle with parsley and serve at once.

Cheesy potato soup

SERVES 4

750 g/1½ lb potatoes, cut into even-sized
　pieces
salt
25 g/1 oz margarine or butter
1 large onion, finely chopped
2 large cloves garlic, finely chopped (optional)
3 celery stalks, finely chopped
1 large carrot, diced small
¼ small swede (weighing about 50 g/2 oz),
　diced small
300 ml/½ pint vegetable stock
150 ml/¼ pint milk
½ teaspoon dried thyme or marjoram
½ teaspoon celery salt
freshly ground black pepper
75 g/3 oz Cheddar cheese, grated
3 tablespoons chopped fresh parsley

1　Cook the potatoes in boiling salted water to cover for about 15 minutes or until tender.

2 When the potatoes are cooked, leave them to cool slightly in the water, then transfer both potatoes and water to a blender and blend until smooth. (If you do not have a blender, pass them through a sieve.) Return the purée to the rinsed-out pan.

3 Melt the margarine in a large frying-pan, add the onion and garlic, if using, and fry over moderate heat until beginning to soften. Add the remaining vegetables to the pan and cook, stirring occasionally, for about 10 minutes, until the vegetables are just beginning to colour.

4 Mix the vegetables with the potato purée in the saucepan, then stir in the stock, milk, thyme and celery salt. Add pepper to taste.

5 Bring to the boil, lower the heat and simmer gently for about 15 minutes or until the vegetables are just soft. Stir in the cheese, reserving 2 tablespoons, and simmer for a further 2-3 minutes. Taste the soup and adjust seasoning.

6 Pour into a warmed soup tureen. Sprinkle with the chopped parsley and the reserved 2 tablespoons grated cheese and serve at once.

Celery and Stilton soup

SERVES 4

1 head celery, finely chopped
100 g/4 oz Stilton cheese, trimmed of rind
40 g/1½ oz butter
2 large leeks, thinly sliced
700 ml/1¼ pints vegetable stock
2 large egg yolks
50 ml/2 fl oz single cream
salt and freshly ground black pepper

To garnish

4 tablespoons vegetable oil
2 slices bread, crusts removed, cubed
4 teaspoons chopped fresh parsley

1 Melt the butter in a large, heavy-based saucepan. Add the celery and leeks, cover and cook gently, stirring occasionally, for about 10 minutes, until the vegetables are softened but not coloured.

2 Add the stock and bring to the boil. Lower the heat and simmer, uncovered, for about 20 minutes, until vegetables are tender. Cool slightly.

Far left: Tomato rice soup
Above: Celery and Stilton soup

3 Meanwhile, make the croûtons: heat the oil in a heavy frying-pan over moderate heat until very hot, add the bread cubes and fry until golden brown on all sides, turning them frequently. Drain on absorbent paper and set aside.

4 Work the slightly cooled vegetable mixture to a purée in a blender. Return the soup to the rinsed-out pan and reheat gently, without boiling.

5 Meanwhile, beat the egg yolks and cream together until smoothly blended. In a separate bowl, mash the cheese to a coarse paste with a fork, then gradually work in the egg and cream mixture.

6 Stir a small ladleful of the hot soup into the cheese mixture, then pour the mixture back into the pan, stirring constantly until the soup has thickened slightly.

7 Pour the soup into 4 warmed individual bowls and garnish each with chopped parsley and the croûtons. Serve at once.

Appetizers

Our tasty appetizers range from unusual vegetable pâtés to exotic fritters – perfect for introducing meals and excellent as melt-in-the-mouth snacks.

Herb pâté

SERVES 6

1 kg/2 lb courgettes
1 tablespoon salt
50 g/2 oz butter
4 eggs
300 ml/¹/₂ pint double cream
2 tablespoons chopped mixed fresh herbs, such as chervil, parsley, mint and tarragon
pinch of cayenne pepper
freshly ground black pepper
vegetable oil, for greasing
hot French bread, to serve

To garnish
3 tablespoons double cream
extra chopped mixed fresh herbs
sprigs of fresh herbs
lettuce leaves
cucumber slices
tomato wedges

1   Coarsely grate the courgettes into a colander. Sprinkle in the salt, stir well and set aside for 1 hour to drain off excess liquid.

2   Rinse the courgettes under cold running water, strain well, then pat dry with absorbent paper.

3   Melt the butter in a saucepan, add the courgettes and cook over a low heat for about 10 minutes, stirring occasionally, until they are soft. Leave to cool.

4   Heat the oven to 180C/350F/Gas 4. Line a 1.5 L/3 pint loaf tin with greaseproof paper, then grease the paper with vegetable oil.

5   Put the eggs and cream in a bowl and mix well. Add the courgette and butter mixture and the herbs. Stir well and season with a pinch of cayenne and black pepper to taste.

6   Pour the mixture into the prepared tin, cover with foil and stand in a roasting tin. Pour enough cold water to come halfway up the sides of the loaf tin.

7   Bake in oven for 1¼ hours until the pâté is firm. Leave the pâté to cool in the tin, then turn out on to a serving dish.

8   To serve: whip the cream until it forms soft peaks, then spread over the top of the pâté. Scatter with chopped mixed fresh herbs and garnish with herb sprigs. Arrange the lettuce leaves, cucumber slices and tomato wedges round the edges of the dish. Serve with hot bread.

Spinach pâté

SERVES 4

225 g/8 oz young spinach leaves, cooked, drained and finely chopped
25 g/1 oz butter
6 spring onions, finely chopped
2 tablespoons chopped fresh mint
1 tablespoon single cream
150 g/5 oz full-fat soft cheese
pinch of cayenne pepper
1 tablespoon lemon juice
salt and freshly ground black pepper
4 thin lemon slices, to garnish
hot granary rolls, to serve

1   Melt the butter in a pan, add the spring onions and fry gently for 2-3 minutes, stirring occasionally. Add the chopped mint and spinach and mix well. Remove from the heat and leave to cool.

2   When the spinach mixture is cool, stir in the cream, cream cheese, cayenne, lemon juice and salt and pepper to taste. Work the mixture in a blender until smooth.

3   Divide the pâté between 4 individual ramekin dishes and smooth the surface of each. Cover and refrigerate for at least 1 hour.

4   To serve: garnish with lemon slices and serve with hot rolls.

Gingered aubergine dip

SERVES 4

1 kg/2 lb firm aubergines, stems removed
175 g/6 oz natural yoghurt
1 clove garlic, crushed
1 tablespoon light soft brown sugar
1 teaspoon grated fresh root ginger
¹/₂ teaspoon cumin powder
salt and freshly ground black pepper
parsley sprigs, to garnish

1   Heat the oven to 200C/400F/Gas 6. Prick the aubergines all over with a fork, then put them into a roasting tin and bake in the oven for 45-60 minutes, until they feel really soft when they are pressed with the back of a spoon.

2   Remove the aubergines from the oven and leave until cool enough to handle. Cut them in half lengthways, and squeeze gently in your hand to drain off the bitter juices. Scoop out flesh and leave until cold.

3   Put aubergine flesh in a blender with the yoghurt, garlic, sugar, ginger, cumin and salt and pepper to taste. Blend until smooth. Transfer to 1 large or 4 small serving dishes. Refrigerate for 2-3 hours to allow dip to firm up.

4   Just before serving, garnish with parsley sprigs.

Luxurious Herb pâté

Lentil and orange purée

SERVES 4

250 g/9 oz split red lentils

600 ml/1 pint water

1 bay leaf

salt and freshly ground black pepper

juice of ½ small orange

2 tablespoons white wine vinegar

4 tablespoons vegetable oil

1 clove garlic, crushed (optional)

4 large celery stalks, finely chopped

2 tablespoons chopped celery leaves (optional)

To garnish

2 small oranges, peeled and cut into segments

350 g/12 oz tomatoes, thinly sliced

celery leaves

1 punnet mustard and cress

1 Put the lentils into a saucepan with the water, bay leaf and salt and pepper to taste. Bring to the boil, then lower the heat, cover and simmer for 45 minutes. Using a wooden spoon, stir occasionally at first, then more frequently towards the end so that the lentils are beaten to a thick purée.

2 Discard the bay leaf, then leave the lentils to cool in the covered pan for 1 hour.

3 Beat the orange juice, vinegar, oil and garlic, if using, into the lentil purée. Taste and adjust seasoning, then mix in the chopped celery and the reserved chopped celery leaves, if using. Stir well.

4 Put the purée into the centre of a serving plate and form it into a smooth mound with the back of a metal spoon. Garnish the purée with the orange segments and arrange the sliced tomatoes and celery leaves around the edge. Arrange the mustard and cress near the tomatoes.

Potted Stilton

MAKES ABOUT 750 G/1½ LB

500 g/1 lb Blue Stilton, rind removed

225 g/8 oz butter

pinch of salt

2 pinches of ground mace

2-4 tablespoons ruby or vintage port

1 Melt 100 g/4 oz of the butter in a small saucepan. Remove from the heat and allow the foam that has developed to fall gently to the bottom of the pan. Pour the clear butter into a bowl, taking care not to disturb the sediment. Set aside.

2 Soften the remaining butter, then put in a mortar and pound with the cheese until evenly blended. Pound in the salt and mace. Work in enough port to give a good flavour and smooth texture: the cheese must not 'weep'.

3 Press the mixture into scalded small pots, tapping on the table while filling to knock out any air-holes. Leave 1 cm/½ inch headspace.

4 Pour the clear butter in a thin layer on top of each pot, then refrigerate overnight.

5 To serve: break and remove the butter coating. The butter-sealed cheese can safely be kept for up to 2 weeks.

Hummus

SERVES 4

100 g/4 oz dried chick-peas

4 tablespoons olive oil

1 large clove garlic, crushed

4 tablespoons lemon juice

4 tablespoons tahini paste

salt and freshly ground black pepper

¼ teaspoon sweet paprika

parsley sprigs and lemon wedges, to garnish

pitta bread, to serve

1 Put the chick-peas into a deep bowl, cover with plenty of cold water and leave to soak for several hours or overnight.

2 Drain and rinse the chick-peas, put them into a saucepan and cover with fresh cold water. Bring to the boil, then simmer for about 1 hour, until tender, adding more water to the pan during the cooking time if the chick-peas become too dry.

3 Drain, reserving the liquid; cool.

4 Reserve 12 chick-peas for garnish. Put the remainder into a blender with half the oil, the garlic, lemon juice, tahini paste and salt and pepper to taste. Blend to a smooth purée, adding a little of the reserved liquid if necessary to give a consistency like thick mayonnaise. Refrigerate the mixture for at least 1 hour.

5 To serve: spoon mixture into a shallow dish, or 4 small individual ones. Put the paprika into a small bowl and gradually stir in the remaining olive oil to make a smooth paste. Drizzle over the humus, garnish with the whole chick-peas, parsley and lemon. Serve with pitta bread.

Spicy bean pâté

SERVES 4

425 g/15 oz can red kidney beans
1 clove garlic, crushed
1 tablespoon tomato purée
1 teaspoon soy sauce
1 teaspoon lemon juice
few drops of Tabasco
salt and freshly ground black pepper
parsley sprigs, to garnish

1 Drain the beans, reserving the liquid from the can.
2 Put all the ingredients into a blender and blend to a smooth paste; it will be flecked with pieces of bean skin. Alternatively, place all the ingredients in a bowl, pound them with the end of a rolling pin, then mash thoroughly

with a fork. If the mixture becomes too thick, add 2-3 tablespoons of the reserved liquid from the can.
3 Taste and adjust seasoning.
4 Pack the pâté into 4 small ramekins or other individual dishes and carefully smooth the surface of each with a small knife. Serve the pâté cold or chilled, garnished with parsley sprigs.

Garlic dip with crudités

SERVES 4-6

250 g/9 oz young French beans, topped and tailed
250 g/9 oz courgettes, cut into 7.5 cm/3 inch matchsticks
1 small cauliflower, broken into florets
250 g/9 oz young carrots, cut into 7.5 cm/3 inch matchsticks
salt

Garlic dip

3-5 cloves garlic
½-¾ teaspoon salt
2 egg yolks, at room temperature
200 ml/7 fl oz olive oil, at room temperature
1-2 teaspoons tepid water
1 teaspoon lemon juice
pinch of freshly ground white pepper

Far left: Lentil and orange purée is delicious served with granary bread Above: Garlic dip with crudités makes a colourful display

1 Blanch the French beans in boiling water for 1 minute, then immediately cool under cold running water, drain and reserve.
2 Dust the courgettes with salt; leave to sweat.
3 Make the dip: crush the peeled garlic cloves and mash to a paste with the salt. Put the egg yolks in a bowl, add the garlic and salt paste, then using a wire whisk or rotary beater, whisk until well combined.
4 Drop by drop, add the oil, beating thoroughly after each addition. When the mixture looks glossy, add the oil a little faster, but do not add too much or the mixture will separate. When the mixture becomes too thick to stir easily, beat in some tepid water.
5 Beat in the lemon juice and pepper to taste. Pour the dip into a small serving bowl and place in the centre of a platter.
6 Rinse courgettes, then drain and pat dry. Surround dip with the courgettes, French beans, cauliflower and carrots and serve.

Avocado dip

SERVES 4-6

2 ripe avocados

juice of 1 lemon

1 clove garlic, crushed (optional)

4 tomatoes, skinned, deseeded and finely chopped

1 small onion, finely chopped

4 tablespoons finely chopped celery

2-3 tablespoons olive oil

1 tablespoon chopped fresh parsley

salt and freshly ground black pepper

To serve

carrot and celery matchsticks

crisps or cheese biscuits

1 Cut the avocados in half lengthways, remove the stones then scoop out the flesh with a teaspoon. Put the flesh in a bowl and mash it with a wooden spoon.

2 Add the lemon juice, garlic, if using, tomatoes, onion and celery.

3 Stir in enough olive oil to make a soft, smooth mixture, then add the chopped parsley and season to taste.

4 Transfer the dip to a serving bowl, cover with cling film and refrigerate for about 30 minutes. Serve with vegetable matchsticks and crisps.

Summer dip

SERVES 6

225 g/8 oz cottage cheese

2 tablespoons natural yoghurt

2 spring onions or ¹/₂ onion

4 gherkins, finely chopped

salt and freshly ground black pepper

dash of Tabasco (optional)

cucumber and celery matchsticks, to serve

1 Sieve or blend the cottage cheese until smooth.

2 Add the yoghurt and mix well.

3 Wash and trim the spring onions. Chop finely and add to the yoghurt mixture. Add the finely chopped gherkins and stir well.

4 Season to taste with salt and pepper and add Tabasco, if using. Cover and refrigerate.

5 Just before serving, give a final stir, transfer to a serving bowl and serve with cucumber and celery sticks.

Hot cauliflower terrine

SERVES 4

1 large cauliflower, broken into florets

salt

50 g/2 oz butter

1 large onion, finely chopped

75 g/3 oz fresh wholemeal breadcrumbs

2 eggs, separated

2 tablespoons finely chopped fresh parsley

1/4 teaspoon freshly grated nutmeg

freshly ground white pepper

150 ml/1/4 pint double cream, lightly whipped

vegetable oil, for greasing

tartare sauce, to serve

1 Heat the oven to 190C/375F/Gas 5 and grease a 1 kg/2 lb loaf tin.

2 Bring a pan of salted water to the boil and cook the cauliflower for 10 minutes until tender. Drain well and mash until smooth.

3 Melt the butter in a pan, add the onion and fry gently for 5 minutes until softened but not coloured. Stir in the cauliflower purée, breadcrumbs, egg yolks, parsley and nutmeg. Season generously with salt and pepper. Whisk the egg whites until standing in stiff peaks and fold them in, together with the cream.

4 Transfer the mixture to the loaf tin, then cover with greased grease-proof or foil. Bake for 1 hour.

5 Leave the terrine in the tin for 3 minutes, then turn out on to a warmed serving dish. Serve with tartare sauce.

Vegetable terrine

SERVES 4

12 large green cabbage leaves, central midribs removed

salt

1 carrot (weight about 100 g/4 oz), cut into matchstick lengths

1 courgette (weight about 100 g/4 oz), cut into matchstick lengths

200 g/7 oz can sweetcorn and pimiento, drained

2 eggs, plus 1 egg yolk

150 ml/1/4 pint milk

3 tablespoons double cream

1/4 nutmeg, grated

freshly ground black pepper

vegetable oil, for greasing

Tomato sauce

250 g/9 oz tomatoes, roughly chopped

3 tablespoons natural yoghurt

1 teaspoon French mustard

1 teaspoon tomato ketchup

pinch of caster sugar

1 Heat the oven to 170C/325F/Gas 3.

2 Bring a saucepan of salted water to the boil and blanch the cabbage leaves for 2 minutes. Drain and dry on a clean tea-towel.

3 Bring a saucepan of salted water to the boil and put the carrot and courgette matchsticks in to simmer for 5 minutes. Drain and refresh under cold water, drain again.

4 Grease a 1 kg/2 lb loaf tin with vegetable oil. Line the loaf tin with 3 or 4 of the largest cabbage leaves and chop the remainder fairly finely.

5 Put half the carrot and courgette mixture into the lined loaf tin, add half the sweetcorn and pimiento, then half the chopped cabbage. Repeat the layering to make 6 layers in all.

6 Whisk the eggs lightly with the extra yolk, milk, cream and nutmeg. Season with salt and pepper. Carefully pour the egg mixture into the loaf tin, gently easing the vegetables apart in several places with a round-bladed knife, to make sure the egg mixture is evenly distributed through the tin and goes right to the bottom. Fold any protruding cabbage leaves over the filling. Cover the tin with foil.

7 Set the loaf tin in a roasting tin. Pour in hot water to come three-quarters up the sides of the loaf tin and cook for 1 1/2-2 hours, until the custard is set and firm to the touch. Remove the loaf tin from the roasting tin and cool. Chill the terrine overnight in the refrigerator.

8 To make the sauce: put the tomatoes in a blender for a few seconds until liquidized, then sieve to remove the skins and seeds.

9 Mix this tomato purée with the remaining sauce ingredients, stirring to make sure they are well combined. Season to taste with salt and pepper. Cover with cling film and chill for at least 2 hours.

10 To serve: allow the terrine to stand at room temperature for about 10 minutes. Run a knife round the sides of the terrine, invert a serving plate on top and shake gently to unmould. Serve cut in slices with the tomato sauce.

Far left: Avocado dip
Below: Vegetable terrine

Egg mousse

SERVES 4

3 hard-boiled eggs, yolks and whites
  separated
2 teaspoons agar-agar
150 ml/1/4 pint vegetable stock
300 ml/1/2 pint thick bottled mayonnaise
1-2 teaspoons curry paste
salt and freshly ground black pepper
1 egg white
parsley sprigs, to garnish

1 Sprinkle the agar-agar over the stock in a small pan, then stir to mix well. Boil until dissolved. Allow to cool slightly, then slowly whisk the mixture into the mayonnaise until smooth.
2 Sieve the egg yolks and stir into the mayonnaise mixture with the curry paste. Chop the egg whites and fold two-thirds of them into the mixture. Season carefully with salt and pepper.
3 Whip the egg white stiffly and fold it into the mixture with a large metal spoon until evenly incorporated. Pour into 4 ramekins that have been rinsed out with cold water.
4 Refrigerate for about 3 hours or until set.
5 To serve: run a knife round the edge of each ramekin and unmould each mousse. Garnish with the remaining chopped egg white and parsley sprigs. Serve at once.

● The mousse can be made in an 850 ml/1½ pint soufflé dish.

Spanish vegetable omelette

SERVES 4

500 g/1 lb potatoes, cut into 1 cm/1/2 inch dice
salt
175 g/6 oz fresh French beans or 100 g/4 oz
  frozen French beans
2 tablespoons vegetable oil
1 onion, chopped
1 red pepper, deseeded and diced
7 eggs, beaten
2 tablespoons finely chopped fresh parsley
1/2 teaspoon sweet paprika
freshly ground black pepper
a little extra finely chopped fresh parsley, to
  garnish

1 Bring a pan of salted water to the boil and cook the potatoes for about 5 minutes, until just tender but not mushy. Drain, refresh in cold water and drain again. Put the potatoes in a large bowl.
2 If using fresh beans, bring a pan of salted water to the boil and cook them for about 8 minutes until tender but still crisp. If using frozen beans, cook for about 5 minutes. Drain, refresh in cold water and drain again. Cut the beans into 2.5-4 cm/1-1½ inch lengths and add to the potatoes in the bowl.
3 Heat the oil in a large non-stick frying-pan, add the onion and red pepper and cook gently for about 5 minutes, stirring occasionally, until softened but not coloured. Remove the onion and pepper from the pan with a slotted spoon, draining all the oil back into the pan, and add to the potatoes and beans.
4 Add the beaten eggs, parsley and sweet paprika to the vegetables in the bowl and stir lightly together. Season to taste with salt and pepper.
5 Reheat the oil in the pan over low heat and pour in the omelette mixture. Level out the vegetables and leave to cook very gently for 15-20 minutes, until the bottom is set but the top is still creamy. Meanwhile, heat the grill to high.
6 Set the frying-pan under the grill at the lowest position from the heat for 2-3 minutes, until the top of the omelette is set and light golden. Loosen the omelette from the pan with a palette knife, then with a fish slice slide it carefully on to a large plate. Sprinkle lightly with chopped parsley and leave to cool slightly. Serve the omelette cut into wedges.

Stuffed eggs with green mayonnaise

SERVES 4

4 large hard-boiled eggs

about ¼ teaspoon lemon juice

pinch of cayenne pepper

½-1 tablespoon finely chopped mixed fresh parsley, watercress and tarragon

Green mayonnaise

15 g/½ oz parsley sprigs

15 g/½ oz watercress sprigs

salt

225 ml/8 fl oz thick bottled mayonnaise

½ tablespoon each finely chopped fresh parsley, watercress and tarragon

freshly ground black pepper

¼-½ teaspoon lemon juice or wine vinegar (optional)

1 Make the green mayonnaise: carefully wash the parsley and watercress sprigs. Bring 300 ml/½ pint salted water to the boil, plunge in the washed herbs and simmer for 6 minutes. Drain well, then pat the herbs as dry as possible in absorbent paper. Put them in a mortar and crush finely, then press through a sieve.

2 Reserve 4 tablespoons of the mayonnaise and blend the rest with the sieved herbs. Stir in the finely chopped parsley, watercress and tarragon and season to taste with freshly ground black pepper, and a little lemon juice or wine vinegar, if liked. Refrigerate until ready to use.

3 Prepare the stuffed eggs shortly before serving, as the filling tends to discolour if left exposed to the air for too long. Carefully shell the hard-boiled eggs. Cut them in half lengthways and scoop out the yolks, taking care not to break the whites.

4 Rub the egg yolks through a fine nylon sieve, then mix well with the reserved mayonnaise and season with the lemon juice and cayenne.

5 Cut a thin slice from the rounded side of each egg white half, if necessary, so that it will stand firmly. Fill each egg white with yolk mixture, piling it up and smoothing it over so that it resembles the whole egg.

6 Spread the green mayonnaise in a shallow rectangular serving dish large enough to take the stuffed eggs side by side. Arrange the eggs on the layer of mayonnaise and sprinkle with the finely chopped mixed green herbs. Serve at once.

Avocado pancakes

MAKES ABOUT 16

1 large firm avocado, peeled and chopped

4 eggs

1 tablespoon milk

1 teaspoon salt

1 onion, chopped

40 g/1½ oz plain flour

1 large potato, grated

1 tablespoon lemon juice

butter, for greasing

Sauce

125 ml/4 fl oz soured cream

150 g/5 oz natural yoghurt

dash of Tabasco

freshly ground black pepper

1 Make the sauce: put the soured cream into a bowl and beat in the yoghurt, Tabasco and black pepper to taste.

2 Put the eggs with milk, salt and chopped onion into the goblet of a blender and blend until thoroughly combined. Add the avocado, flour, potato, lemon juice and black pepper to taste and blend for a few seconds at low speed.

3 Heat oven to 110C/225F/Gas ¼.

4 Heat a heavy frying-pan over a moderate heat, lightly grease with butter and pour in about 50 ml/2 fl oz of the batter. Cook until the underside is lightly browned, then turn the pancake over and cook until browned on the other side. Carefully lift on to a sheet of greaseproof paper and keep warm.

5 Continue making pancakes in the same way, interleaving them with greaseproof paper.

6 Serve the pancakes with the sauce handed separately.

Far left: Egg mousse and toast fingers
Below: Stuffed eggs with green mayonnaise

Egg and spinach nests

SERVES 4

4 eggs

250 g/9 oz spinach, stalks and large midribs removed, shredded

25 g/1 oz margarine or butter

salt and freshly ground black pepper

4 tablespoons double cream

cayenne pepper, to garnish

margarine, for greasing

buttered wholemeal toast, to serve

1 Heat the oven to 190C/375F/Gas 5. Grease 4 individual ovenproof dishes or ramekins.
2 Melt the margarine in a saucepan, add the spinach and cook gently for 8 minutes, or until soft. Season to taste with salt and pepper.
3 Divide the spinach between the prepared dishes. Break 1 egg into each dish on top of the cooked spinach mixture.
4 Place the dishes on a baking sheet and bake in oven for 10 minutes, until the egg whites begin to set. Remove from the oven and spoon 1 tablespoon cream over each egg. Return to the oven and cook for a further 5 minutes.
5 Sprinkle a little cayenne over each egg and serve at once accompanied by buttered wholemeal toast.

Egg and avocado bake

SERVES 6

6 eggs, separated

1 large avocado

6 tablespoons browned breadcrumbs

3 tablespoons vegetable oil

1 onion, finely chopped

1 clove garlic, crushed (optional)

4 tablespoons finely chopped fresh parsley

salt and freshly ground black pepper

75 g/3 oz Cheddar cheese, grated

melted margarine, for greasing

finely chopped fresh parsley or coriander, to garnish

1 Heat the oven to 200C/400F/Gas 6. Brush 6 individual ovenproof dishes with melted margarine, then coat them evenly with 4 tablespoons of the breadcrumbs. Shake out the excess crumbs. Set aside.

2 Heat the oil in a frying-pan, add the onion and garlic, if using, and fry gently for 3-4 minutes until the onion is soft but not coloured. Set aside to cool for about 5 minutes.

3 Cut the avocado in half. Remove the stone, scoop out the flesh into a bowl, then mash with a fork to a purée. Beat in the egg yolks and parsley, then the cooled onion and salt and pepper to taste.

4 Beat the egg whites until standing in stiff peaks, then fold them into the avocado mixture. Pile into the dishes, scatter remaining crumbs on top and bake in the oven for 20 minutes.

5 Sprinkle the top of the rising mixture with the cheese, then return dishes to the oven for a further 15 minutes until they are well risen and golden.

6 Garnish with finely chopped parsley and serve at once.

Tomatoes with cheese filling

SERVES 4

8 fairly large, firm ripe tomatoes
150 g/5 oz full-fat soft cheese
150 g/5 oz curd cheese
2 tablespoons top of the milk or single cream
2 tablespoons finely chopped fresh parsley
2 teaspoons tomato purée
salt and freshly ground black pepper
8 sprigs of parsley, to garnish

Dressing

6 tablespoons vegetable oil
2 tablespoons wine vinegar
1/2 teaspoon mustard powder
1/2 teaspoon dried basil
2 teaspoons caster sugar

1 Slice the tops off the tomatoes and reserve. Scoop out the seeds and core.

Far left: Egg and spinach nests
Above: Tomatoes with cheese filling

2 Put the cheeses in a bowl with the top of the milk or cream, parsley, tomato purée and salt and pepper to taste. Blend together smoothly. Spoon the mixture into tomatoes, piling it high, and replace the reserved tomato lids at an angle.

3 Place the stuffed tomatoes in a shallow dish. Beat together the dressing ingredients with a fork, adding salt and pepper to taste. Spoon the dressing over the tomatoes and chill in refrigerator for at least 30 minutes.

4 To serve: put 2 tomatoes on each of 4 plates. Beat the dressing remaining in the dish together again and sprinkle 1 teaspoon of the dressing over each tomato. Tuck a sprig of parsley beneath the lid of each tomato to garnish.

Italian stuffed mushrooms

SERVES 4

16 large mushrooms
100 g/4 oz frozen finely chopped spinach
1 tablespoon olive oil
50 g/2 oz butter
1 small onion, finely chopped
1 clove garlic, crushed
*100 g/4 oz Ricotta cheese or sieved cottage
   cheese*
4 tablespoons grated Parmesan cheese
4 tablespoons fresh wholemeal breadcrumbs
salt
freshly ground black pepper
parsley sprigs, to garnish
garlic bread, to serve

1   Heat the oven to 180C/350F/Gas 4. Cook the spinach according to the instructions on the packet.

2   Meanwhile, remove the stalks from the mushrooms and set aside. (Use the mushroom stalks for making stock.) Heat the oil and half the butter in a frying-pan, add the onion and garlic, and fry them gently for 5 minutes until the onion is soft and lightly coloured. Remove from the heat.

3   Put the cooked spinach in a bowl with the Ricotta, Parmesan and bread-crumbs. Stir in the onion and garlic, together with the buttery juices left in the pan, and season to taste with salt and pepper.

4   Place the mushrooms, gills upper-most, in an ovenproof dish and divide the stuffing equally between them. Dot with the remaining butter and bake in the oven for 15 minutes.

5   Using a fish slice, transfer the mushrooms to 4 warmed individual serving plates, garnish with sprigs of parsley and serve at once with garlic bread.

Above: Italian stuffed mushrooms
Far right: Braised stuffed artichokes

Chinese lettuce parcels

SERVES 6

6 large crisp lettuce leaves
2 tablespoons vegetable oil
4 spring onions, finely chopped
1 teaspoon ground ginger
1 celery stalk, finely chopped
75 g/3 oz mushrooms, finely chopped
*50 g/2 oz canned water chestnuts, drained
   and finely sliced*
100 g/4 oz long-grain rice, cooked
100 g/4 oz frozen peas, cooked and drained
1½ tablespoons soy sauce
1 egg beaten
extra soy sauce, to serve

1 Dip the lettuce leaves in boiling water for 10 seconds to soften, then drain on absorbent paper.

2 Heat the oil in a wok or large frying-pan. Add the spring onions and ginger and fry gently for 2-3 minutes until soft.

3 Add the celery, mushrooms and water chestnuts and fry for a further 5 minutes.

4 Stir in the rice, peas and soy sauce. Remove the pan from the heat and stir in the egg.

5 Lay the lettuce leaves out flat on a work surface. Put about 2 generous tablespoons of the mixture at the base of each lettuce leaf. Fold the leaf around the mixture and roll up to form neat parcels. Secure with cocktail sticks, if necessary.

6 Place the parcels in a steamer. If you do not have a steamer, use a metal colander which fits neatly inside a saucepan (the base must not touch the water). Fill the pan with boiling water, place the parcels in the colander and place the colander in the pan. Cover with foil or lid of steamer and steam for 5 minutes.

7 Remove the cocktail sticks from the parcels, if using, then place the parcels on a warmed serving dish. Serve at once, with extra soy sauce handed separately.

Braised stuffed artichokes

SERVES 4

4 globe artichokes
salt
1/2 lemon
1 tablespoon lemon juice
25 g/1 oz butter
300 ml/1/2 pint dry white wine
1 onion, finely chopped
2 carrots, quartered

Stuffing

50 g/2 oz butter
50 g/2 oz mushrooms, finely chopped
50 g/2 oz fresh wholemeal breadcrumbs
2 tablespoons chopped fresh parsley
2 teaspoons dried mixed herbs
2 cloves garlic, crushed
finely grated zest of 1 lemon
freshly ground black pepper

1 Bring a large pan of salted water to the boil.

2 Meanwhile, prepare artichokes: using a sharp knife, neatly cut off the artichoke stalks, then slice off the top third of each artichoke. Discard the trimmings. Rub the cut surfaces with the lemon to prevent discoloration.

3 Using scissors, trim any remaining sharp tips from the leaves, rub with lemon, then open them to expose the central whiskery 'choke', surrounded by purple leaves. Pull out the purple leaves, then scoop out the hairy chokes with a teaspoon and discard.

4 Add the lemon juice to the boiling water and then add the artichokes and cook for 15-20 minutes or until an outer leaf of the artichokes can be pulled out quite easily.

5 Meanwhile, make the stuffing: melt the butter in a saucepan, add the mushrooms and fry gently for 5 mi-nutes until soft and lightly coloured. Transfer to a bowl and stir in remaining stuffing ingredients. Season to taste with salt and pepper and mix.

6 Drain the artichokes, then stand upside down in a colander to extract all the water.

7 Heat the oven to 180C/350F/Gas 4.

8 Stand the artichokes upright and spoon the stuffing into the centres. Place in an ovenproof dish, then put a knob of butter on top of each.

9 Pour the wine around the artichokes, then add the onion and carrots to the wine. Season lightly with salt and pepper, cover the dish with foil and cook in the oven for about 40 minutes.

10 Serve at once, straight from the dish: pour a little of the wine sauce over each serving.

Spinach soufflés

SERVES 4

500 g/1 lb fresh spinach or 250 g/9 oz frozen chopped spinach

salt

50 g/2 oz margarine or butter

1 onion, finely chopped

25 g/1 oz plain flour

150 ml/¼ pint milk

good pinch of freshly grated nutmeg

freshly ground black pepper

4 eggs, separated

1 tablespoon grated Parmesan cheese

margarine, for greasing

1 If using fresh spinach, wash very thoroughly and remove the stalks and central midribs. Place the spinach in a saucepan with only the water that clings to the leaves, and sprinkle with salt. Cover and cook over moderate heat for about 10 minutes until the spinach is cooked, stirring occasionally. If using frozen spinach, cook according to packet instructions.

2 Drain the spinach well in a sieve, pressing out all the excess water. Chop the spinach, if using fresh. Grease four

300 ml/½ pint soufflé dishes. Heat the oven to 190C/375F/Gas 5.

3 Melt the margarine in a large saucepan, add the onion and cook over low heat for about 5 minutes until soft and lightly coloured. Sprinkle in the flour and stir over low heat for 1-2 minutes until straw-coloured. Remove from the heat and gradually stir in the milk. Return to moderate heat and simmer, stirring until thick.

4 Stir in the chopped spinach and grated nutmeg and season well with salt and pepper. Simmer over gentle heat for 2 minutes.

5 Remove from the heat. Beat the egg yolks and beat them into the spinach mixture.

6 Whisk the egg whites until they are just standing in soft peaks then beat 1-2 tablespoons into the spinach mixture. Carefully fold the rest of the whites into the mixture.

7 Pour the mixture into the greased soufflé dishes and sprinkle the tops evenly with the grated Parmesan cheese. Bake in the oven for 20-30 minutes until risen and lightly browned on the top. They should be firm to the touch on the outside, and not wobbly if gently shaken, but still moist in the centre. Serve at once.

Above: Spinach soufflés
Far right: Mixed vegetables à la grecque

Asparagus with walnuts

SERVES 4

500 g/1 lb asparagus, trimmed

salt

4 tablespoons walnut oil

pinch of cayenne pepper

50 g/2 oz walnuts, finely chopped

4 tablespoons finely chopped fresh parsley or coriander

1 Tie the asparagus into 4 bundles. Bring a deep pan of salted water to the boil and put in the asparagus, leaving the tips above the water. Cover with the lid or a dome of foil and boil gently for 15 minutes until tender.

2 Drain the asparagus and put each bundle on a warmed individual plate. Remove the strings.

3 Spoon walnut oil over each bundle and sprinkle with a little cayenne pepper. Divide the chopped walnuts and the parsley between the plates and serve at once.

Potato gnocchi and tomato sauce

SERVES 4

750 g/1½ lb potatoes
100 g/4 oz plain flour
25 g/1 oz butter, softened
pinch of freshly grated nutmeg
1 egg yolk, beaten
50 g/2 oz Parmesan cheese, grated
butter, for greasing
Tomato sauce
1 small onion, finely chopped
1 clove garlic, crushed (optional)
150 g/5 oz can tomato purée
300 ml/½ pint water
1 teaspoon sugar
1 bay leaf
pinch of dried basil
salt and freshly ground black pepper

1 Make the sauce first: place all the ingredients in a pan with salt and pepper to taste. Bring to the boil, then lower the heat, cover and simmer gently for 30 minutes.
2 Meanwhile, bring the potatoes to the boil in salted water, lower the heat and cook for 20 minutes until tender. Drain, then pass through a sieve into a bowl.
3 Work the sauce through a sieve, then return to the rinsed-out pan. Set aside. Grease an ovenproof dish and heat oven to 110C/225F/Gas ¼.
4 Beat the flour into the potatoes with the butter, nutmeg and salt and pepper to taste. Add just enough of the beaten egg yolk to bind the mixture. Work in 40 g/1½ oz of the grated Parmesan.
5 Bring a large pan of lightly salted water to a simmer.
6 Meanwhile, turn the potato mixture on to a floured surface, divide into 3 and form each piece into a roll about 2.5 cm/1 inch in diameter. Cut each roll into 2.5 cm/1 inch slices.
7 Drop slices from 1 roll into the simmering water. Cook for about 5 minutes, or until they rise to the surface and look puffy. Remove with a slotted spoon, place in the prepared dish and keep hot in the oven while you cook the remaining pieces in the same way.
8 Reheat the tomato sauce. Heat the grill to high.
9 Pour a little of the warmed tomato sauce over the gnocchi and top with the remaining Parmesan. Place under the grill for about 5 minutes until the top is golden and bubbling. Serve at once, with the remaining sauce handed separately in a warmed jug.

Mixed vegetables à la grecque

SERVES 4

250 g/9 oz small button onions
350 g/12 oz frozen green beans, defrosted
175 g/6 oz button mushrooms, thickly sliced
salt
2 tablespoons chopped fresh parsley
Sauce
6 tablespoons dry white wine or dry cider
4 tablespoons olive oil
4 tablespoons tomato purée
1 onion, thinly sliced
1 clove garlic, finely chopped
1 teaspoon mustard seed or pickling spice
freshly ground black pepper

1 Bring a large pan of salted water to the boil and blanch the small onions for 3 minutes. Drain the onions thoroughly.
2 Make the sauce: put the wine, oil, tomato purée, sliced onion, garlic and mustard seed into a saucepan. Stir well and bring to the boil, then lower the heat, cover the pan and simmer over very low heat for 25 minutes, stirring the sauce once or twice. Season the sauce to taste with salt and freshly ground black pepper.
3 Add the whole onions, beans and sliced mushrooms to the sauce and return to the boil. Cover the pan and simmer for 20 minutes until the vegetables are tender. Taste and adjust seasoning, if necessary.
4 Remove from the heat and leave to cool, then transfer to a covered container. Stir in most of the parsley and refrigerate for 30 minutes.
5 To serve: sprinkle with remaining parsley to garnish and serve.

Above: Cheesy potato fritters
Far right: Melted Mozzarella sandwiches

Oriental vegetable fritters

SERVES 4

1 large cauliflower, broken into bite-sized
  florets
2 bunches large spring onions, trimmed and
  halved lengthways
500 g/1 lb carrots, halved lengthways and cut
  into 6 cm/2¹/2 inch lengths
vegetable oil, for deep-frying

Batter

100 g/4 oz plain flour
¹/4 teaspoon bicarbonate of soda
¹/4 teaspoon salt
¹/4 teaspoon ground ginger
1 egg yolk
200 ml/7 fl oz water

Dipping sauce

3 tablespoons tomato purée
1¹/2 tablespoons soy sauce
1¹/2 tablespoons clear honey
4 tablespoons vegetable stock

1 Make the dipping sauce: stir together the ingredients for the sauce, then divide the mixture between 4 tiny dishes or ramekins. Set aside.
2 Make the batter: sift the flour, bicarbonate of soda, salt and ginger into a bowl. Beat the egg yolk with the cold water and add gradually to the flour, stirring with a wooden spoon, to make a smooth thin batter.
3 Heat the oven to 130C/250F/Gas ¹/2. Heat the oil in a deep-fat frier to 190C/375F, or until a cube of bread browns in 50 seconds.
4 Dip a few vegetable pieces into the thin batter. Transfer them to the hot oil with a slotted spoon and deep-fry for about 3 minutes or until golden brown, turning once with the spoon. Remove from the pan with the slotted spoon and drain well on absorbent paper. Arrange on a warmed large serving platter and keep warm in the oven while frying the remaining vegetable pieces in the same way.
5 Serve the fritters as soon as they are all cooked: provide each person with a bowl of sauce so that they can dip their vegetables into it.

Cheesy potato fritters

MAKES 20-24

1 kg/2 lb potatoes
100 g/4 oz full-fat soft cheese, flavoured with
  garlic and herbs
2 eggs
salt and freshly ground black pepper
vegetable oil, for frying
1 tablespoon snipped chives, to garnish
  (optional)

1 Grate the potatoes, then drain them in a colander lined with a tea-towel. Gather the tea-towel up and squeeze out as much liquid from the potatoes as possible.
2 Put the cheese into a bowl and beat with a wooden spoon until soft. Beat in the eggs, then mix in the potatoes and season the fritter mixture with salt and freshly ground black pepper to taste.
3 Heat the oven to 110C/225F/Gas ¹/4.
4 Pour enough oil into a deep frying-

pan to cover the base to a depth of 2.5 cm/1 inch. Heat the oil over moderate heat until sizzling hot, then fry the potato mixture in batches: drop tablespoons of the mixture into the oil, spacing them well apart. Fry for about 3 minutes on each side until golden brown.

5 Remove from the pan with a slotted spoon, drain on absorbent paper, then transfer to a serving dish. Keep hot in the oven while frying the remaining mixture in the same way. Serve the fritters as soon as they are all cooked, garnished with the snipped chives, if liked.

Melted Mozzarella sandwiches

SERVES 4

100 g/4 oz Mozzarella cheese
8 large slices white or wholemeal bread
50 g/2 oz butter, softened
freshly ground black pepper
3 eggs, beaten
vegetable oil, for frying
parsley sprigs, to garnish

1 Spread the bread with the butter and cut off the crusts with a sharp knife. Season 4 of the bread slices with pepper.
2 Cut the Mozzarella into thin slices and arrange them in a single layer on the seasoned bread, leaving a 5 mm/¼ inch margin all round the edge of the bread.
3 Top with the remaining 4 bread slices. Press the edges firmly together.
4 Put beaten eggs on a plate and dip in each sandwich to coat thoroughly all over. Make sure that the edges are well covered with egg so that they are sealed.
5 Heat the oven to 110C/225F/Gas ¼. Pour enough oil into a large frying-pan to come to a depth of 5 mm/¼ inch. Heat gently until a bread cube sizzles and turns golden brown when dropped into the oil.
6 Fry 2 of the sandwiches for 3-4 minutes on each side until evenly golden brown.
7 Drain very thoroughly on absorbent paper. Keep warm in the oven while frying the remaining sandwiches. Serve at once, garnished with parsley sprigs.

Cheese beignets

SERVES 4

3 eggs, separated
¼ teaspoon salt
50 g/2 oz butter
6 tablespoons plain flour
250 ml/8 fl oz water
vegetable oil, for deep-frying
175 g/6 oz Gruyère cheese, grated
25 g/1 oz Parmesan cheese, grated

1 Beat the egg yolks till frothy. In a clean, dry bowl, whisk the egg whites until they stand in stiff peaks.
2 Melt the butter in a small saucepan. Sprinkle in the flour and stir over low heat for 1-2 minutes. Gradually stir in the water and simmer, stirring, until thick and smooth. Remove from the heat.
3 Heat the oil in a deep-fat frier to 180C/350F; or until a stale bread cube browns in 60 seconds.
4 Beat the Gruyère cheese into the hot sauce. Fold in the whisked whites.
5 Fry 1 tablespoon of batter, a few at a time, turning once with a slotted spoon. When golden, remove and leave to drain on absorbent paper. Sprinkle with grated Parmesan.

Walnut croquettes

MAKES ABOUT 16

100 g/4 oz shelled walnuts, very finely chopped
75 g/3 oz fresh wholemeal breadcrumbs
1/2 small onion, grated
50 g/2 oz Edam cheese, finely grated
1 tablespoon finely chopped fresh parsley
salt and freshly ground black pepper
1 large egg, lightly beaten
1-2 tablespoons milk
2 tablespoons vegetable oil, for frying

Sauce

15 g/1/2 oz margarine or butter
150 g/5 oz frozen spinach
150 ml/1/4 pint soured cream
freshly grated nutmeg

1   Put the walnuts in a bowl with the breadcrumbs, onion, cheese, parsley and salt and pepper to taste. Stir in the beaten egg, then add just enough milk to bind the mixture together. Form into about 16 balls, using your hands.
2   To make the sauce: melt the margarine in a small saucepan, add the spinach and heat gently for about 10 minutes until defrosted, stirring frequently. Drain thoroughly in a sieve, pressing out the liquid with a saucer, then chop with a knife. Return to the pan, stir in the soured cream, then season to taste with nutmeg and salt and pepper. Set aside.
3   Heat the oil in a frying-pan, add the croquettes and fry carefully for about 10 minutes, turning them frequently until brown on all sides.
4   Meanwhile, gently heat the sauce until hot, but do not boil. Spoon the sauce into a warmed serving bowl and place in the centre of a large platter. Arrange the croquettes on the platter around the sauce, and serve at once.

Mushroom and cheese pirozhki

MAKES 24

100 g/4 oz mushrooms, finely chopped
25 g/1 oz butter
1 spring onion, finely chopped
75 g/3 oz full-fat soft cheese, flavoured with garlic and herbs
1/2 teaspoon dillweed
salt and freshly ground black pepper
shortcrust pastry, made with 100 g/4 oz wholemeal flour (page 42)
1 egg yolk, lightly beaten, to glaze
vegetable oil, for greasing
parsley sprigs, to garnish

1   Heat the oven to 180C/350F/Gas 4 and grease a baking sheet with oil.
2   Melt the butter in a frying-pan and gently fry the mushrooms and spring onion for 3 minutes. Remove from heat and cool.
3   In a clean, dry bowl, mash the soft cheese with the dillweed. Stir in the mushrooms and spring onion, season to taste with salt and pepper, then refrigerate.
4   Meanwhile, roll out the pastry on a lightly floured work surface to a 5 mm/1/4 inch thickness. Using a round pastry cutter or the rim of a glass, cut out circles approximately 8 cm/3½ inches in diameter.
5   Place 1 teaspoonful of the mushroom and cheese mixture on one half of each circle, taking care not to overfill the pastry circles or they will be very difficult to seal. Fold into a crescent shape and seal edges with water. Continue until all are filled.
6   Place crescents on prepared baking sheet and then brush each one with a little egg yolk to glaze. Bake in the oven for 30-40 minutes until the pastry is cooked and golden in colour. Transfer to a warmed serving plate, garnish with the parsley sprigs and serve.

French onion flan

SERVES 6

2 large onions, finely chopped

100 g/4 oz butter

1 tablespoon plain flour

3 eggs

150 ml/¼ pint single cream

150 ml/¼ pint double cream

pinch of freshly grated nutmeg

salt and freshly ground black pepper

finely sliced onion rings or parsley sprigs, to
   garnish

Cheese pastry

175 g/6 oz plain flour

½ teaspoon mustard powder

½ teaspoon salt

pinch of cayenne pepper

100 g/4 oz butter, diced

75 g/3 oz mature Cheddar cheese, finely
   grated

1 large egg yolk, lightly beaten

4-5 teaspoons water

1 Make the pastry: sift the flour, mustard powder, salt and cayenne pepper into a bowl. Add the butter and rub into the dried ingredients with your fingertips, until the mixture resembles fine breadcrumbs. Stir in the cheese. Mix to a stiff paste with the egg yolk and water.

2 Turn the dough out on to a lightly floured surface and knead gently until smooth. Wrap the dough in cling film and chill for at least 30 minutes.

3 Heat the oven to 200C/400F/Gas 6.

4 Roll out the dough on a lightly floured surface and use to line a 23 cm/9 inch loose-based flan tin or ring set on a baking sheet. Prick the base of the dough all over with a fork. Line the pastry case with foil and fill it with baking beans. Bake in the oven for 10 minutes, then remove from the oven. Turn down the oven to 180C/350F/Gas 4.

5 Remove the foil and beans, then bake the pastry case for a further 5 minutes. Remove from oven; allow the

*Far left: Mushroom and cheese pirozhki
are excellent with thin soup
Above: French onion flan has a rich
cheese pastry case*

pastry case to cool slightly.

6 Meanwhile, make the filling: melt the butter in a small pan, add the onions and fry gently for 10 minutes until soft. Remove the pan from the heat and allow the onions to cool.

7 Stir in the flour, then beat together the eggs and single and double cream and beat into the onion mixture. Add the nutmeg and season to taste with salt and pepper.

8 Turn down the oven to 170C/325F/Gas 3. Pour the filling into the pastry case and bake for 35-40 minutes, until set and golden brown.

9 Allow the flan to cool for about 5 minutes, then carefully remove from the tin and transfer to a serving plate. Garnish with a few onion rings and serve warm or cold.

Tomato, cheese and basil flan

SERVES 4-6

4 large tomatoes, each weighing about 250 g/
*   9 oz, sliced*

300 ml/½ pint milk

3 large eggs

1½ teaspoons dried basil

75 g/3 oz mature Cheddar cheese, grated

freshly ground black pepper

a few tomato slices, to garnish (optional)

Wholemeal shortcrust pastry

100 g/4 oz wholemeal flour

½ teaspoon baking powder

pinch of salt

50 g/2 oz margarine or butter, diced

2-3 tablespoons water

1 Make the pastry: sift the flour with the baking powder and salt, then tip the bran left in the sieve on to the flour and stir in well. Add the margarine and rub into the flour with your fingertips until the mixture resembles fine breadcrumbs. Mix in just enough cold water to form a soft ball. Wrap the dough in cling film and refrigerate for 30 minutes.

2 Heat the oven to 190C/375F/Gas 5.

3 Roll out the pastry on a floured surface and use to line a 20 cm/8 inch loose-based flan tin or flan ring set on a baking sheet.

4 Arrange the tomato slices overlapping in the flan case. In a bowl, whisk together the milk, eggs, basil, 50 g/ 2 oz of the cheese and salt and pepper to taste.

5 Pour the mixture into the flan case and sprinkle over the remaining cheese. Bake in the oven for 40-45 minutes until the filling is set and golden brown on top.

6 Allow the flan to cool for 5 minutes, then carefully remove from tin and transfer to a serving plate. Garnish the edge with tomato slices, if liked. Serve warm or cold.

Right: Tomato, cheese and basil flan is
full of flavour and goodness
Far right: Watercress flan has a light-
weight cottage cheese filling

Spinach nut pasties

MAKES 8

350 g/12 oz frozen spinach, defrosted

3 tablespoons vegetable oil

2 onions, chopped

25 g/1 oz porridge oats

100 g/4 oz mixed shelled nuts, finely
*   chopped*

2 teaspoons soy sauce

salt and freshly ground black pepper

shortcrust pastry, made with 225 g/8 oz
*   wholemeal flour (see left)*

vegetable oil, for greasing

1 Make the filling: heat the oil in a pan, add the onions and fry gently for 5 minutes until soft and lightly coloured. Add the porridge oats and continue cooking for about 5 minutes until lightly coloured. Remove from the heat and stir in the spinach, nuts and soy sauce. Season with salt and pepper to taste, then leave until completely cold.

2 Heat the oven to 200C/400F/Gas 6. Lightly grease a baking sheet with vegetable oil.

3 Divide the pastry into 8 equal portions and roll out each portion to a 10 cm/4 inch round. Using a tablespoon, divide the spinach filling be-

tween the pastry circles, placing it in the middle of each one.

4 Brush halfway round the pastry edges with water. Gently lift the pastry sides and bring them up to meet in the middle and enclose the filling completely. Seal the edges firmly and crimp.

5 Arrange the pasties on the prepared baking sheet. Prick the tops of the pasties and cover the baking sheet with foil. Bake in the oven for 25-30 minutes until crisp and lightly browned. Serve hot or cold.

Watercress flan

SERVES 6

2 bunches of watercress, finely chopped
shortcrust pastry, made with 100 g/4 oz
 wholemeal flour (page 42)
350 g/12 oz cottage cheese, sieved
3 eggs, beaten
3 tablespoons milk
pinch of cayenne pepper
salt and freshly ground black pepper
lightly beaten egg white, to seal
watercress sprigs, to garnish

1 Heat the oven to 200C/400F/Gas 6.
2 Roll out the pastry on a lightly floured surface and use to line a 23 cm/9 inch flan tin. Prick base with fork. Place a large circle of greaseproof paper or foil in the pastry case and weight it down with baking beans. Bake for 10 minutes.
3 Remove the paper or foil lining and beans, brush the pastry case with beaten egg white, then return to the oven for a further 5 minutes.
4 Meanwhile, make the filling: put the sieved cottage cheese into a large bowl, add the chopped watercress, beaten eggs and milk and mix well with a fork. Add the cayenne and season with salt and pepper.
5 Spoon the filling into the cooked pastry case and spread evenly.
6 Return to the oven for about 35 minutes, or until the filling has set and is golden brown on top. Serve, garnished with the watercress sprigs.

Brie quiche

SERVES 4-6

shortcrust pastry, made with 100 g/4 oz
 wholemeal flour (page 42)
lightly beaten egg white, to seal
watercress sprigs, to garnish

Filling
250 g/9 oz Brie cheese, rind removed,
 reserved and cut into 2.5 cm/1 inch squares
150 ml/1/4 pint single cream
3 eggs
1/2 teaspoon light soft brown sugar
pinch of ground ginger
pinch of ground turmeric
pinch of salt

1 Heat the oven to 200C/400F/Gas 6.
2 On a lightly floured surface, roll out the pastry to line a 20 cm/8 inch loose-based flan tin or flan ring set on a baking sheet. Prick the base lightly with a fork. Place a large circle of greaseproof paper or foil in the pastry case and weight it down with baking beans. Bake in the oven for 10 minutes.
3 Remove the beans and paper or foil, brush the inside of the pastry case with beaten egg white and return the pastry case to the oven for a further 5 minutes to crispen slightly.
4 Meanwhile, put the cheese in a blender with the remaining filling ingredients and blend until smooth.
5 Lower the oven temperature to 180C/350F/Gas 4. Arrange the squares of Brie rind over the base of the pastry case and pour over the filling. Bake in the oven for 30-40 minutes, until the filling is set and brown. The squares of rind rise to the top of the filling and melt to form a golden crust over the top of the quiche.
6 Allow the quiche to cool for about 5 minutes, then carefully remove from tin and transfer to a serving plate. Garnish the centre with watercress sprigs and serve warm or cold.

Main Courses

**Vegetables, grains, eggs and cheese are miraculously
transformed into delicious vegetarian main courses. Plan your
menu around the main course to ensure a well-balanced meal.**

Cauliflower and oat casserole

SERVES 4

1 cauliflower, broken into florets
100 g/4 oz rolled oats
salt
2 tablespoons plain flour
300 ml/½ pint soured cream
1 teaspoon French mustard
175 g/6 oz mature Cheddar cheese, grated
freshly ground black pepper
250 g/9 oz button mushrooms, trimmed
25 g/1 oz butter
50 g/2 oz coarsely chopped walnuts

1 Heat the oven to 200C/400F/Gas 6. Put the cauliflower florets in a saucepan containing 2.5 cm/1 inch boiling salted water and cook for about 7 minutes, or until they are just tender. Drain well
2 Meanwhile, put the flour in a small bowl and blend to a smooth paste with a little of the soured cream. Gradually stir in the remaining soured cream, the mustard, half the grated cheese and salt and freshly ground black pepper to taste.
3 Mix in the cauliflower and mushrooms, turning gently so that all the vegetables are coated. Pour into a shallow ovenproof dish.
4 Using a fork, mix the butter with the oats, then add the rest of the cheese and the walnuts to make a lumpy, crumbly mixture.
5 Sprinkle the oat mixture evenly over the cauliflower and mushrooms and bake for 40 minutes until the topping is golden brown and crisp. Serve at once.

Ratatouille

SERVES 6

3 large aubergines, halved lengthways
3 large courgettes, halved lengthways
salt
150 ml/¼ pint olive oil
3 large onions, sliced into thin rings
4 tablespoons tomato purée
4 cloves garlic, chopped
3 large peppers, deseeded and cut into strips
5 large tomatoes, skinned and chopped
1 tablespoon chopped fresh coriander
small pinch of cinnamon
1 teaspoon chopped fresh basil
freshly ground black pepper

1 Cut the aubergines and courgettes across into slices about 2 cm/¾ inch thick, then arrange them in layers in a colander, sprinkling each layer with salt. Top with a weighted plate and leave to drain for 1 hour.
2 Heat the oil in a large heavy-based pan over low heat, add the onions and fry gently for about 10 minutes until soft but not coloured. Stir in the tomato purée and cook for 3-4 minutes, stirring occasionally.
3 Rinse aubergines and courgettes in cold water, then pat dry with absorbent paper and add to pan. Stir in the garlic and peppers, cover and simmer for 20 minutes.
4 Add the tomatoes and the rest of the seasoning, stir, and leave to cook for a further 40-45 minutes. Remove the lid for the final few minutes to let the sauce reduce if the dish seems too liquid. Taste and adjust the seasoning before serving.

Bulgarian vegetable stew

SERVES 4

100 g/4oz dried white haricot beans, soaked overnight
100 g/4oz whole brown lentils, soaked overnight
2 tablespoons vegetable oil
2 large onions, chopped
2 teaspoons ground cumin
2 teaspoons ground coriander
4 large red peppers, deseeded and sliced
1 L/1¾ pints unsalted vegetable stock or water
4 tablespoons tomato purée
50 g/2 oz currants
salt and freshly ground black pepper
sugar

1 Heat the oil in a large flameproof casserole, add the onions, cumin and coriander and fry gently for 5 minutes, until soft. Add the peppers and cook gently for 4-5 minutes, stirring from time to time.
2 Drain the haricot beans and boil rapidly in water for 10 minutes; drain. Drain the lentils, then add with the beans to the onions and peppers. Stir well, then pour in the vegetable stock. Add the tomato purée and currants and stir well.
3 Bring to the boil, then lower the heat and simmer, half-covered, for 1-1¼ hours, until the lentils and beans are tender and the sauce is thickened.
4 Season to taste with salt and pepper and a little sugar. Serve hot.

Hearty Bulgarian vegetable stew

Vegetable hotpot

SERVES 4

25 g/1 oz margarine or butter
1 large onion, thinly sliced
250 g/9 oz carrots, sliced
600 ml/1 pint hot vegetable stock or water
1 tablespoon tomato purée
bouquet garni
salt and freshly ground black pepper
250 g/9 oz leeks, sliced
100 g/4 oz parsnips, diced
250 g/9 oz potatoes, cut into chunks
grated Cheddar cheese, to serve

1 Melt the margarine in a large saucepan, add the onion and fry gently for 5 minutes, until soft and lightly coloured. Add the carrots and stir for 1 minute. Pour on the stock, add the tomato purée and bouquet garni and season to taste with salt and pepper. Stir well to mix.
2 Bring to the boil, cover, lower the heat slightly and simmer gently for 10 minutes.
3 Add the leeks and parsnips and cook for a further 10 minutes. Add a little extra boiling water if the sauce seems to be drying out.
4 Add the potatoes to the saucepan, cover and cook for a further 30 minutes, or until all the vegetables are tender.
5 Discard the bouquet garni, taste the stock and adjust the seasoning. Transfer the vegetables to a warmed serving dish and serve at once with the grated Cheddar cheese handed separately in a small bowl.

Vegetable crumble

SERVES 4

2 tablespoons olive oil or sunflower oil
2 leeks, cut into 1 cm/½ inch slices
2 large carrots, thickly sliced
1 small red pepper, deseeded and diced
500g/1 lb courgettes, cut into 1 cm/½ inch slices
400g/14 oz can tomatoes
½ teaspoon dried basil
salt and freshly ground black pepper
25-50g/1-2 oz pine nuts
2 teaspoons wine vinegar

Crumble topping

100 g/4 oz plain or wholemeal flour
¼ teaspoon salt
40g/1½ oz butter, diced
65g/2½ oz fresh Parmesan cheese, grated

1 Heat the oil in a large saucepan, add the leeks and carrots and fry over moderate heat for 5 minutes, stirring. Add the red pepper and fry for 5 minutes, then add courgettes and fry for a further 5 minutes, stirring constantly.
2 Add the tomatoes and their juices to the pan with the basil and salt and pepper to taste. Bring to the boil, then lower the heat, cover and simmer for 10 minutes.
3 Meanwhile, heat the oven to 200C/400F/Gas 6 and make the crumble: sift the flour and salt into a bowl. Add the butter and rub into the flour with the fingertips until the mixture resembles fine breadcrumbs. Stir in 50 g/2 oz of the Parmesan, and add pepper to taste.
4 Add the pine nuts and vinegar to the vegetables, then transfer to a 1.5 L/2½ pint casserole. Sprinkle the crumble evenly over vegetables, then top with remaining Parmesan.
5 Bake for about 40 minutes. Serve.

Vegetables in curry sauce

SERVES 4

1 small cauliflower, broken into florets
250 g/9 oz small carrots, scraped and thickly
  sliced
250 g/9 oz French beans, trimmed and cut
  into chunks
250 g/9 oz shelled broad beans
salt
Sauce
25 g/1 oz butter
25 g/1 oz plain flour
1 tablespoon mild curry powder
large pinch of ground ginger
300 ml/½ pint milk
2 tablespoons fresh orange juice
freshly ground black pepper
2 tablespoons single cream or top of the milk
1 tablespoon blanched almonds, halved and
  toasted
1 tablespoon finely chopped fresh mint or
  parsley

1 Heat the oven to 110C/225F/Gas ¼
2 Bring a large pan of boiling salted water to the boil, add all the prepared vegetables and cook until they are just tender – no more than 10 minutes. Do not allow the vegetables to become soft.
3 Drain the vegetables, reserving the stock. Transfer the drained vegetables to a warmed serving dish and keep hot in the oven.
4 Make the sauce: melt the butter in a saucepan, sprinkle in the flour and stir over low heat to form a paste. Stir in the curry powder and ginger and cook over moderate heat for 3 minutes, stirring constantly.
5 Remove the pan from the heat and gradually stir in the milk, orange juice and 300 ml/½ pint of the reserved stock. Return to the heat and simmer, stirring, for 3 minutes until thickened and smooth. Taste the sauce and season with pepper, and salt if necessary. Remove the pan from the heat and stir in the cream.
6 Pour the sauce over the vegetables, lightly tossing them with a fork to coat well. Scatter with the almonds and chopped mint or parsley and serve at once.

● To toast the almonds, spread the nuts out in a grill pan and grill under moderate heat until golden, shaking the pan occasionally.

Creamy spring vegetables

SERVES 4

50 g/2 oz butter
1 small onion, sliced
2 large spring onions, cut into 1 cm/½ inch
  slices
2 carrots, cut into 1 cm/½ inch slices
300 ml/½ pint hot vegetable stock
pinch of caster sugar
salt and freshly ground black pepper
250 g/9 oz broad beans (shelled weight)
250 g/9 oz peas (shelled weight)
1 teaspoon cornflour
6 tablespoons double cream

1 Melt the butter in a saucepan, add the sliced onion and spring onions and cook over moderate heat for 2 minutes. Add the sliced carrots and cook for a further 2 minutes, stirring to coat thoroughly.
2 Pour the hot stock into the pan,

Far left: Vegetable hotpot is based on a variety of root vegetables
Above: Creamy spring vegetables marry well with plain brown rice

add the sugar and salt and pepper to taste, then bring to the boil. Lower the heat, cover and simmer gently for 10 minutes. Add the broad beans and simmer for a further 5 minutes. Add the peas and continue simmering for another 10 minutes, until all the vegetables are tender.
3 Put the cornflour into a small bowl and stir in 1 tablespoon of the hot liquid from the pan. Stir to make a smooth paste, then pour back into the pan. Stir the contents of the pan over low heat for about 4-5 minutes, until the sauce thickens and clears. Stir in the cream and allow just to heat through.
4 Turn the vegetables with the sauce into a warmed serving dish and serve at once.

Pumpkin stew

Vegetable cobbler

Above: Pumpkin stew
Right: Fruit curry

SERVES 4

500 g/1 lb pumpkin, peeled, deseeded and cut into 2 cm/³/4 inch cubes

3 tablespoons vegetable oil

1 onion, chopped

250 g/9 oz carrots, thinly sliced

100 g/4 oz red lentils

400 g/14 oz can tomatoes

300 ml/¹/2 pint vegetable stock

¹/2 teaspoon ground mace

salt and freshly ground black pepper

150 ml/¹/4 pint soured cream, to serve

1 Heat the oil in a saucepan and fry onion and carrots over moderate heat for 5 minutes.

2 Add the lentils, tomatoes with their juice, stock and mace, and season with salt and pepper to taste. Bring to the boil, lower the heat, cover the pan and simmer gently for 15 minutes.

3 Add the pumpkin to the pan, cover and then simmer gently for a further 15 minutes.

4 Taste and adjust the seasoning if necessary. To serve: spoon the stew into warmed individual bowls, top each serving with a spoonful of soured cream and serve at once.

SERVES 4-6

500 g/1 lb Jerusalem artichokes, peeled and cut into 2.5cm/1 inch chunks

salt

50 g/2 oz margarine or butter

1 onion, finely sliced

100 g/4 oz mushrooms, sliced

40 g/1¹/2 oz plain flour

300 ml/¹/2 pint milk

100 g/4 oz Cheddar cheese, grated

freshly ground black pepper

250 g/9 oz tomatoes, skinned and quartered

Topping

175 g/6 oz wholemeal flour

1 tablespoon baking powder

¹/2 teaspoon salt

40 g/1¹/2 oz margarine or butter, diced

25 g/1 oz shelled walnuts, finely chopped

³/4 teaspoon dried mixed herbs

about 150 ml/¹/4 pint milk

1 Put the artichokes in a saucepan, cover with water and add a good pinch of salt. Bring to the boil, lower the heat slightly and simmer for 5-10 minutes until just tender. Drain, re-serving the liquid.

2 Melt the margarine in a saucepan, add the onion and fry gently for 5 minutes until soft and lightly coloured. Add the mushrooms and continue cooking for 5 minutes. Transfer the vegetables to a plate.

3 Sprinkle the flour into the pan and stir over low heat for 1-2 minutes. Remove from the heat and gradually stir in 150 ml/¹/4 pint of the reserved artichoke liquid and the milk. Return to the heat and simmer, stirring, until the sauce is thick and smooth. Reserve 1 tablespoon of the cheese and stir the rest into the sauce. Season to taste with salt and pepper.

4 Stir in the artichokes, onion and mushrooms and tomatoes. Taste and adjust the seasoning, then turn the vegetable mixture into a 1.5 L/2¹/2 pint casserole.

5 Heat the oven to 220C/425F/Gas 7.

6 Make the scone topping: sift the flour, baking powder and salt into a large bowl. Tip the bran left in the sieve into the bowl and stir well to mix. Add the margarine and rub it in with the fingertips until the mixture resembles fine breadcrumbs. Add the walnuts and herbs and gradually mix in enough milk to form a soft dough.

7 Turn the dough on to a lightly

floured surface and roll out thinly. Cut into about 15 rounds using a 5 cm/2 inch cutter and arrange these on top of the casserole. Sprinkle with the reserved cheese.

8 Bake the casserole in the oven for about 30 minutes or until the scone topping has risen and is golden brown. Serve at once.

Mixed bean casserole

SERVES 4-6

100 g/4 oz haricot beans
100 g/4 oz brown beans or borlotti
100 g/4 oz black-eyed beans
1 green pepper, deseeded
2 tablespoons vegetable oil
1 large onion, chopped
1 small head of celery, chopped
2 cloves garlic, crushed (optional)
793 g/1 lb 12 oz can tomatoes
425 ml/¾ pint water
1 teaspoon yeast extract
2 teaspoons dried oregano
salt and freshly ground black pepper

1 Put the haricot beans into 1 bowl and the brown and black-eyed beans together in another. Cover both of them with cold water and leave to soak overnight.

2 Drain the haricot, brown and black-eyed beans, rinse them under cold running water, then put into a medium-sized saucepan and cover with fresh cold water.

3 Bring to the boil and then boil for 15 minutes to remove any toxins. Lower the heat slightly, cover the pan and continue cooking for a further 30 minutes.

4 Meanwhile, cut a few slices from the green pepper and reserve for the garnish. Chop the remaining pepper. Heat the oil in a large heavy-based pan and gently fry the onion, celery, the chopped green pepper and garlic, if using, for 10 minutes. Add the tomatoes and water, then stir in the yeast extract, oregano and salt and freshly ground black pepper to taste. Bring to the boil.

5 Drain the beans, add to the pan of vegetables, cover and cook gently for 1 hour or until the beans are very tender. Taste and adjust the seasoning, if necessary.

6 Transfer the beans to a warmed serving dish and serve at once, garnished with the reserved green pepper rings linked together.

Fruit curry

SERVES 4

50 g/2 oz block of creamed coconut, broken into pieces
2 tablespoons curry paste
150 ml/¼ pint soured cream
1 banana
½ honeydew melon, cut into 2.5cm/1 inch cubes
100 g/4 oz each green and black grapes, halved and deseeded
1 orange, divided into segments
1 red dessert apple, cored (do not peel)
plain boiled rice, to serve

1 Put the coconut, curry paste and soured cream into a large saucepan. Stir over low heat until the mixture is well blended.

2 Peel the banana, cut into 1 cm/½ inch slices and add to pan with the melon, grapes and orange. Cook gently, stirring, for 3-4 minutes until the fruit is warm.

3 Cut the apple into small wedges and remove cores. Stir into the pan and warm through.

4 Spoon the curry on to a bed of boiled rice and serve at once.

Country goulash

Above: Country goulash
Far right: Rich potato pie

Beetroot slice

SERVES 4

2 tablespoons vegetable oil

2 onions, sliced

2 carrots, sliced

2 celery stalks, sliced

2 courgettes, sliced

1 green pepper, deseeded and diced

50 g/2 oz mushrooms, sliced

500 g/1 lb white cabbage, finely shredded

400 g/14 oz can tomatoes

1 tablespoon tomato purée

1 teaspoon lemon juice

300 ml/1/2 pint water

41/2 teaspoons sweet paprika

1 tablespoon caraway seeds

salt and freshly ground black pepper

150 ml/1/4 pint soured cream

1 Heat the oil in a large saucepan, add the onions, carrots and celery and

fry for about 5 minutes until soft and lightly coloured.

2 Add courgettes, green pepper, mushrooms and white cabbage and cook over moderate heat for 10 minutes, stirring occasionally to prevent the vegetables sticking to the saucepan.

3 Stir in the tomatoes with their juices, the tomato purée, lemon juice and water. Sprinkle in the paprika and caraway seeds and stir gently. Season well with salt and freshly ground black pepper.

4 Cover the pan and simmer for 20 minutes or until the vegetables are just tender. Taste and add more seasoning if necessary.

5 Transfer the goulash to a hot serving dish and spoon over the soured cream. Serve at once.

SERVES 4-6

100 g/4 oz plain flour

100 g/4 oz wholemeal flour

1/4 teaspoon salt

100 g/4 oz margarine or butter, diced

4-6 teaspoons iced water

Filling

175 g/6 oz Lancashire cheese, grated

175 g/6 oz cooked beetroot, skinned and coarsely grated

1 small onion, finely grated

1 teaspoon French mustard

2 tablespoons thick bottled mayonnaise

1 tablespoon sweet pickle

salt and freshly ground black pepper

1 Make the pastry: sift both flours into a bowl with the salt. Tip the bran left in the sieve into the bowl and stir to mix. Add the margarine or butter and rub into the flours with your fingertips until the mixture resembles fine crumbs. Add the water gradually and mix well to make a fairly firm dough that is not too dry and crumbly. Wrap the dough in cling film and refrigerate for 30 minutes.

2 Heat the oven to 200C/400F/Gas 6.

3 Meanwhile, make the filling: in a bowl mix together the cheese, beetroot, onion, French mustard, mayonnaise, pickle and salt and pepper to taste.

4 Roll out half the pastry on a lightly floured surface and use to line a shallow 18 cm/7 inch square tin. Roll out the remaining pastry into a square slightly larger than the top of the tin and set aside.

5 Spread the filling over the pastry in the tin. Dampen the edges of the pastry with water, then lay the reserved pastry square over the top. Press it on to the side of the pastry lining above the level of the filling, then trim level with the top of the tin.

6 Brush with cold water, sprinkle lightly with salt, then make a hole in the top for the steam to escape. Bake just above the centre of the oven for 30-35 minutes, or until the pastry is crisp and light golden.

7 Serve hot, warm or cold, cut into slices or squares.

Rich potato pie

SERVES 6

500 g/1 lb plain flour

1½ teaspoons salt

200 g/7 oz butter, diced

2 eggs, separated

5 tablespoons water

margarine, for greasing

Filling

1 kg/2 lb waxy potatoes

salt and freshly ground black pepper

4 tablespoons chopped fresh parsley

2 tablespoons chopped fresh chervil or 2 teaspoons dried chervil

175 g/6 oz finely chopped shallots

150 ml/¼ pint double cream, lightly whipped

1 Sift the flour and salt into a bowl and rub in the butter until the mixture resembles breadcrumbs. Lightly whisk one whole egg and one egg white with 4 tablespoons water, add to the dry ingredients and mix with a knife until the dough leaves the sides of the bowl clean. Wrap the dough in cling film and refrigerate for about 30 minutes.

2 Meanwhile, cook the potatoes for 5 minutes in a large pan of boiling, salted water. Drain well, and when cool enough to handle, cut into slices.

3 Heat the oven to 200C/400F/Gas 6. Grease a 23 cm/9 inch deep flan tin.

4 Roll out slightly more than half the pastry on a lightly floured surface and use to line the prepared tin.

5 Arrange a third of the potato slices in the pastry case, season lightly with salt and pepper and sprinkle over half the herbs and shallots. Cover with another third of the potato slices, season and sprinkle with the rest of the herbs and shallots, then cover with the remaining potato.

6 Beat the remaining egg yolk with 1 tablespoon water and use to brush the pastry edges. Roll out the remaining pastry into a round slightly larger than the top of the tin, then place over the filled tin. Trim and seal the edges. Brush with the remaining egg yolk mixture and cut 4 small steam vents, spaced evenly, in the top of the pie.

7 Bake in the oven for 25 minutes, then reduce the temperature to 180C/350F/Gas 4 and cook for 20 minutes.

8 Remove the pie from the oven and open the steam vents sufficiently with a sharp knife to take a small funnel. Pour one quarter of the cream into each of the steam vents and return the pie to the oven for a further 10 minutes, or until the top is rich golden brown. Serve at once.

Bulgur wheat casserole

SERVES 4

225 g/8 oz bulgar wheat
50 g/2 oz butter
1 tablespoon vegetable oil
1 large onion, finely chopped
2 large leeks, thinly sliced
2 large carrots, diced
1 red pepper, deseeded and diced
300 ml/½ pint boiling water
2 tomatoes, skinned and chopped
50 g/2 oz seedless raisins
100 g/4 oz Cheddar cheese, diced
salt and freshly ground black pepper

1 Melt half the butter with the oil in a large heavy-based saucepan. Add the onion, leeks, carrots and red pepper, cover and cook gently for about 20 minutes.
2 Meanwhile, melt the remaining butter in a large saucepan. Add the bulgur wheat and stir gently until the grains are thoroughly coated with the butter.
3 Stir in the boiling water, cover and place over gentle heat. Cook for 10 minutes until the water has been absorbed.
4 Using a fork, gently mix the cooked vegetables into the bulgur wheat. Lightly stir in the tomatoes, seedless raisins and diced cheese and fork through until the cheese is melted. Season to taste with salt and freshly ground black pepper.
5 Transfer the casserole to a warmed serving dish and serve at once.

Above: Bulgur wheat casserole
Far right: Nutty rissoles

Chestnut wine loaf

SERVES 4-6

350 g/12 oz dried chestnuts or 1 kg/2 lb fresh chestnuts
50 g/2 oz butter, plus extra for greasing
1 large onion, chopped
2 celery stalks, finely chopped
2 cloves garlic, crushed
2 tablespoons chopped fresh sage
1 tablespoon red wine
1 egg
salt and freshly ground black pepper
1 sage leaf, to garnish (optional)

1 If using dried chestnuts, cover them with boiling water, leave to soak for at least 2 hours, then simmer in plenty of water for about 1½ hours until tender. For fresh chestnuts, nick each one with a knife, then simmer the chestnuts in plenty of water for about 10 minutes until the cuts open. Remove the chestnuts from the water one by one and strip off the skins with a sharp, pointed knife. Put the skinned chestnuts into a saucepan, cover with water and simmer for 20-30 minutes until tender. Drain and mash the chestnuts.

2 Heat the oven to 180C/350F/Gas 4. Line the base and narrow sides of a 500 g/1 lb loaf tin with a long strip of silicone paper; brush with butter.

3 Melt the butter in a large saucepan, add the onion and celery and fry gently for 10 minutes until soft but not coloured. Remove from the heat. Add the mashed chestnuts, garlic, sage, wine and egg and mix well. Season with salt and pepper to taste.

4 Place the sage leaf, if using, in the base of the prepared loaf tin and spoon the chestnut mixture on top. Smooth over the surface with a palette knife and cover with a piece of foil.

5 Bake the loaf in the oven for 1 hour. To serve: slip a knife round the sides of the loaf and turn it out on to a warmed serving dish. Serve the loaf at once.

Nutty rissoles

MAKES 12

225 g/8 oz mixed unsalted nuts, finely chopped
25 g/1 oz butter
175 g/6 oz onions, finely chopped
1 large clove garlic, crushed (optional)
175 g/6 oz mushrooms, finely chopped
100 g/4 oz fresh wholemeal breadcrumbs
1 tablespoon finely chopped fresh parsley
2 teaspoons dried mixed herbs
2 tablespoons tomato purée
1 teaspoon soy sauce
1 egg, beaten
salt and freshly ground black pepper
3-4 tablespoons plain flour, for coating
vegetable oil, for frying
mushroom slices and walnut halves, to garnish
fried onion rings and tomato sauce (page 37), to serve

1 Melt the butter in a saucepan, add the onions and garlic, if using, and fry over gentle heat for 4-5 minutes until soft.

2 Remove the pan from the heat and stir in the nuts, mushrooms, breadcrumbs, parsley and mixed herbs until well blended. Add the tomato purée and soy sauce and sufficient beaten egg to bind the mixture together. Season to taste with salt and pepper.

3 Roll heaped tablespoons of the mixture in flour to form 12 balls, then flatten them into rissoles about 7.5cm/ 3 inches in diameter.

4 Arrange the prepared rissoles on a floured baking sheet and leave in the refrigerator or in a cold place for about 1 hour.

5 Heat the oven to 110C/225F/Gas ¼.

6 Heat a little vegetable oil in a large frying-pan and fry half the rissoles, cooking them for about 5 minutes on each side or until crisp and golden brown. Remove with a slotted spoon; drain on absorbent paper. Put them in the oven to keep warm while cooking the remaining rissoles.

7 When all the rissoles are cooked, garnish with mushroom slices and walnut halves and serve them at once, with onion rings and tomato sauce.

Mixed vegetable croquettes

MAKES 16

1 tablespoon vegetable oil
2 onions, very finely chopped
6 celery stalks, very finely chopped
2 carrots, grated
175 g/6 oz mushrooms, very finely chopped
1 tablespoon smooth peanut butter
75 g/3 oz unsalted peanuts, ground or very finely chopped
75 g/3 oz fresh wholemeal breadcrumbs
pinch of dried mixed herbs
salt and freshly ground black pepper
2 eggs, beaten
75 g/3 oz dried breadcrumbs
vegetable oil, for deep-frying

1 Heat the oil in a large saucepan, add the onions and celery and fry gently for 5 minutes. Do not allow the vegetables to brown.
2 Add the carrots and mushrooms to the pan and continue cooking for a further 5 minutes, stirring occasionally.
3 Remove from the heat, then stir in the peanut butter until well combined. Add the peanuts, wholemeal breadcrumbs, herbs and salt and pepper to taste. Mix well and bind with half the beaten eggs. Leave until cool
4 Meanwhile, pour the remaining beaten eggs into a shallow bowl or on to a plate. Place the dried breadcrumbs on a separate plate, ready to coat the croquettes.
5 When the mixture is cool, divide it into 16 portions and shape them into croquettes. Dip each croquette in the beaten eggs, then roll in the breadcrumbs until thoroughly coated.
6 Pour enough vegetable oil into a deep-fat frier to come to a depth of 4 cm/1½ inches. Heat to 180C/350F or until a 2.5 cm/1 inch bread cube browns in 60 seconds. Lower in the croquettes and deep-fry for 3 minutes, until golden brown. Drain the croquettes very thoroughly on absorbent paper and serve at once.

Below: Mixed vegetable croquettes
Far right: Potato pizza

Soya burgers

SERVES 4

175 g/6 oz soya beans
2 tablespoons vegetable oil
1 onion, finely chopped
1 small carrot, grated
1 small green pepper, deseeded and chopped
1 tablespoon tomato purée
1 teaspoon dried mixed herbs
salt and freshly ground black pepper
1 egg
1 tablespoon water
dried breadcrumbs, for coating
vegetable oil, for frying

1 Put the beans into a bowl, cover with plenty of cold water and leave to soak overnight. Drain the soaked beans and put them into a saucepan; cover with cold water.
2 Bring the beans to the boil, then lower the heat and simmer over very gentle heat for 3 hours until tender, topping up with more water if necessary. Transfer to a colander and drain thoroughly.
3 Heat the oil in a frying-pan and gently fry the onion and carrot for 5 minutes, until the onion is soft and lightly coloured. Add the green pepper and fry for a further 5 minutes, until the vegetables are just tender.
4 Add the beans, tomato purée and herbs to the pan, mashing the beans with a spoon to make the mixture hold together. Season with salt and pepper.
5 Divide the mixture into 8 and shape each piece into a neat, flat circle. Beat egg and water together in a shallow bowl and spread breadcrumbs out on a plate. Dip the burgers first into the beaten egg mixture, then into the dried breadcrumbs, making sure they are well coated.
6 Heat the oven to 110C/225F/Gas ¼.
7 Heat the vegetable oil in a large frying-pan, add 4 burgers and fry over moderately high heat for 3 minutes on each side until crisp and browned. Place on a serving platter, and keep warm. Fry the remaining burgers in the same way and serve at once.

Potato pizza

SERVES 4

250 g/9 oz cold mashed potatoes
125 g/4 oz self-raising flour
salt
50 g/2 oz margarine or butter
vegetable oil, for greasing

Topping

1 tablespoon vegetable oil
1 large onion, sliced
1 red pepper, deseeded and sliced
1 clove garlic, crushed (optional)
125 g/4 oz button mushrooms, sliced
pinch of oregano
2 teaspoons malt vinegar
freshly ground black pepper
1 tablespoon tomato purée
175 g/6 oz Cheddar cheese, sliced
12 green olives, stoned (optional)

1 Heat the oven to 230C/450F/Gas 8. Grease a large baking sheet.
2 Make the base: sift the flour and salt into a large bowl. Add the margarine and rub it in with your fingertips until the mixture resembles breadcrumbs, then add the mashed potatoes and knead the mixture lightly until smooth.
3 Press the dough into a 25 cm/10 inch round and refrigerate.
4 Meanwhile, make the topping: heat the oil in a frying-pan, add the onion, red pepper and garlic, if using, and fry gently for 5 minutes or until the onion is soft and lightly coloured. Remove the pan from the heat and stir in the mushrooms, oregano, vinegar and salt and pepper to taste.
5 Place the potato base on the baking sheet and spread the tomato purée over it, then top with the onion mixture. Arrange the cheese slices over the top and top with stoned olives, if liked.
6 Bake in the oven for 25-30 minutes or until the base is firm and the cheese is golden brown. Serve at once.

● For a more Italian flavour, use Mozzarella cheese instead of Cheddar and top with black olives.

Carrot and nut roast

SERVES 4

250 g/9 oz carrots, coarsely grated
100 g/4 oz cashew nuts or pieces
100 g/4 oz walnut pieces
100 g/4 oz granary or wholemeal bread
50 g/2 oz margarine or butter
1 onion, finely chopped
6 tablespoons hot vegetable stock
2 teaspoons yeast extract
1 teaspoon clear honey
1 teaspoon dried mixed herbs
2 teaspoons lemon juice
salt and freshly ground black pepper
margarine or butter, for greasing

1 Heat the oven to 180C/350F/Gas 4. Grease an 850 ml/1½ pint shallow ovenproof dish. Grind the cashews, walnuts and bread together in batches in a blender until they are all fairly fine. Tip them into a bowl.
2 Melt the margarine in a saucepan, add the onion and fry gently for 5 minutes until soft and lightly coloured. Add the carrots and cook, stirring, for a further 5 minutes. Remove from the pan with a slotted spoon and add to the nuts and bread in the bowl.
3 Put the hot stock in a bowl, add the yeast extract and honey and stir until dissolved. Stir into the nut mixture with the herbs and lemon juice. Taste the mixture and season with salt and pepper.
4 Spoon mixture into prepared dish and bake in the oven for 45 minutes. Serve the roast hot or cold, straight from the ovenproof dish.

Herb and spinach crêpes

SERVES 4-6

50 g/2 oz plain flour
½ teaspoon salt
2 eggs, beaten
150 ml/¼ pint milk
4-6 tablespoons water
5 tablespoons melted butter
225 g/8 oz frozen finely chopped spinach, defrosted
2 tablespoons finely chopped fresh basil, chives or tarragon
2-4 tablespoons grated Parmesan cheese
vegetable oil, for frying
butter, for greasing
tomato sauce (page 37), to serve

Filling

500 g/1 lb cottage cheese
125 ml/4 fl oz soured cream
2 eggs, beaten
50 g/2 oz Gruyère cheese, grated
2-4 tablespoons grated Parmesan cheese
2-4 tablespoons finely chopped fresh herbs (parsley, chives and, when available, tarragon)
salt and freshly ground black pepper
freshly grated nutmeg

1 Make the batter: sift the flour and salt into a bowl, then make a well in the centre. Beat in the eggs, then gradually add the milk, water and 2 tablespoons of the melted butter. Stir gently until smooth.
2 Strain the batter through a fine sieve; it should be the consistency of single cream. Add a little water if too thick. Stir in the spinach and herbs and leave to stand for two hours.
3 Make the filling: put the cottage cheese in a bowl with the soured cream, eggs, Gruyère and Parmesan cheese and the herbs. Season to taste with salt, pepper and nutmeg. Refrigerate for 1 hour.
4 Make the crêpes: heat a little oil in a heavy-based 18 cm/7 inch frying-pan over moderate to high heat. Pour off the excess. Whisk the batter.
5 Remove the pan from the heat, pour about 2 tablespoons batter into the pan, then tilt the pan to spread the batter all over the base.

6 Return to the heat and cook until the underside is golden brown, then turn the crêpe and cook on the other side for a further 20-30 seconds until golden brown. Lift on to a sheet of greaseproof paper.
7 Continue making crêpes in this way, greasing the pan with more oil if necessary. Stack by interleaving with greaseproof paper.
8 Heat the oven to 180C/350F/Gas 4. Spread each crêpe with 4-5 tablespoons of the filling, then roll up the crêpes and arrange in a greased baking dish.
9 Brush the crêpes with the remaining melted butter and sprinkle with the grated Parmesan cheese. Bake for about 20 minutes, until the crêpes are heated through. Serve at once, with tomato sauce.

Nutty brown rice

SERVES 4

250 g/9 oz brown rice
600 ml/1 pint water
1 teaspoon salt
2 tablespoons vegetable oil
1 large onion, chopped
2 celery stalks, finely chopped
1 bunch spring onions, trimmed and chopped
1 red-skinned dessert apple, cored and chopped
50 g/2 oz raisins
50 g/2 oz flaked almonds
50 g/2 oz roasted peanuts
steamed spinach, to serve

Cheese sauce

40 g/1½ oz butter
25 g/1 oz flour
300 ml/½ pint milk
1 tablespoon mild, wholegrain mustard
100 g/4 oz Cheddar cheese, grated
freshly ground black pepper

1 Put the rice, water and salt in a heavy-based saucepan and bring to the boil. Stir once, cover, and cook over a gentle heat for 40-50 minutes, or until the rice is tender and all the water has been absorbed.
2 Meanwhile, make the sauce: melt two-thirds of the butter in a saucepan, sprinkle in the flour and stir over low heat for 1-2 minutes until straw-coloured. Remove from the heat and gradually stir in the milk. Return to the heat and simmer, stirring until thick and smooth. Stir in the mustard and cheese and season to taste with salt and pepper. Dot the remaining butter over the top of the sauce and set aside.
3 Heat the oil in a frying-pan, add the onion and celery and fry gently for 10 minutes, taking care not to let them brown. Add the spring onions and cook for a further 2 minutes.
4 Mix the vegetables into the cooked rice with a fork, then stir in the apple, raisins, almonds and peanuts. Heap the mixture on to a warmed serving dish and keep warm while you reheat the sauce, stirring in the butter on its surface.
5 To serve: surround the rice with a ring of spinach, pour the sauce over the rice and serve at once.

Moors and Christians

Spicy vegetable pilau

SERVES 6

2 onions
2.5 cm/1 inch piece fresh root ginger
3 cardamom pods
3 cloves
2.5 cm/1 inch piece of cinnamon
50 g/2 oz butter
1 small cauliflower, broken into florets
1 bay leaf (optional)
3-4 carrots, cut into matchstick strips
50 g/2 oz shelled peas
400 g/14 oz basmati rice, rinsed and drained
800 ml/28 fl oz water
1 tablespoon sugar
salt
2 hard-boiled eggs, quartered, to garnish

1 Slice 1 of the onions lengthways very thinly and reserve. Chop the other onion with the ginger and reserve. Crush the cardamom pods, cloves and cinnamon with a rolling pin and reserve.

2 Heat 1 tablespoon of the butter in a deep frying-pan or saucepan over moderate heat. When hot, fry the cauliflower florets until they are light brown, then remove with a slotted spoon and set aside.

3 Add the rest of the fat to the pan and fry the onion slices until they are browned, remove from the pan and set aside.

4 In the same fat, gently fry the onion and ginger mixture and the bay leaf, if using, until the onion is soft and lightly coloured. Stir in the reserved spices, carrot strips and the peas, then add the rice and fry for about 5 minutes until it becomes transparent.

5 Add the water to the pan, together with the sugar and salt to taste. Bring the water to the boil, then simmer for about 10 minutes or until the rice is half cooked.

6 Add the reserved cauliflower and continue cooking until the water is absorbed and the rice and vegetables are tender but not mushy. Transfer to a warmed serving dish.

7 Serve the pilau hot, garnished with the onion slices and the hard-boiled egg quarters.

Moors and Christians

SERVES 4-6

225 g/8 oz black beans, soaked overnight and drained
2 tablespoons vegetable oil
1 onion, chopped
1 clove garlic, crushed
1 green pepper, deseeded and thinly sliced
1 red pepper, deseeded and thinly sliced
2 large tomatoes, skinned, deseeded and chopped
250 g/9 oz long-grain rice
600 ml/1 pint water
large pinch of cayenne pepper
salt and freshly ground black pepper
25 g/1 oz butter
4-6 large eggs
1 tablespoon chopped parsley

1 Rapidly boil the beans in unsalted water for 10 minutes, then simmer for 1 hour.

2 Heat the oil in a saucepan, add the onion and garlic and fry gently for 3 minutes until soft but not coloured. Add the sliced peppers, stir well and fry for a further 3 minutes, stirring occasionally. Do not allow the vegetables to brown.

3 Add the tomatoes, rice, water, drained beans, cayenne pepper and salt and pepper to taste. Stir well, cover the pan and simmer very gently for about 45 minutes, until the rice is tender and the liquid has been absorbed. Taste and adjust the seasoning if necessary.

4 Heat the oven to 110C/225F/Gas ¼.

5 Turn the rice mixture on to a warmed serving dish and keep warm. Heat the butter in a frying-pan and fry the eggs.

6 To serve: divide the rice between 4-6 warmed serving plates and top each portion with a fried egg. Sprinkle each egg with parsley and serve at once while hot.

and juice. Remove from heat.

8 Line the base and sides of the dish with half the blanched cabbage leaves, arranging them so that they overlap and allowing them to overhang the dish. Stir the cheese and egg into the rice mixture, season to taste with salt and pepper, then spoon into the lined dish. Level the surface of the mixture and cover with the remaining leaves. Fold over the overhanging leaves.

9 Cover the dish tightly with foil and cook for 45 minutes.

10 Loosen the sides with a knife and turn out on to a warmed plate.

Marrow with nut stuffing

SERVES 4

1.25 kg/2³/4 lb whole marrow

salt

4 tablespoons vegetable oil

1 large onion, finely chopped

1 clove garlic, finely chopped

100 g/4 oz fresh wholemeal breadcrumbs

75 g/3 oz peanuts, skinned and ground

75 g/3 oz cashew nuts, ground

2 tablespoons finely chopped fresh parsley

1 tablespoon finely chopped fresh marjoram

1 tablespoon tomato purée

6 tablespoons dry white wine

freshly ground black pepper

vegetable oil, for greasing

1 Heat the oven to 200C/400F/Gas 6. Lightly grease a casserole large enough to hold the marrow in one piece.

2 Cut off both ends of the marrow and reserve. Scoop and discard the seeds from the main part.

3 Put the marrow and both reserved ends into a large saucepan of lightly salted boiling water, return to the boil and simmer for 5 minutes. Drain well.

4 Heat the oil in a frying-pan over a low-heat, add the onion and garlic and fry gently for 5 minutes until soft but not coloured.

5 Remove the pan from the heat and mix in the breadcrumbs, nuts, herbs, tomato purée and wine. Season to taste with salt and pepper.

6 Fill the marrow with the stuffing, then fix the end pieces back in place with cocktail sticks. Place the marrow in the casserole, cover and cook in the oven for 1 hour.

7 To serve, discard the ends and cut the marrow into 4 thick slices.

Stuffed cabbage pie

SERVES 4-6

1 green cabbage, weighing about 1 kg/2 lb

1 orange

salt

175 g/6 oz long-grain rice

15 g/1/2 oz margarine or butter

1 onion, chopped

1 cooking apple, weighing about 150 g/5 oz

50 g/2 oz stoned dates, chopped

75 g/3 oz Cheddar cheese, grated

1 egg, beaten

freshly ground black pepper

margarine, for greasing

1 Grate the zest of half the orange and squeeze the juice from the whole orange. Reserve.

2 Heat the oven to 180C/350F/Gas 4 and grease an ovenproof dish 20 cm/8 inches in diameter and 7.5 cm/3 inches deep.

3 Bring a pan of salted water to the boil and cook the rice for about 10 minutes until just tender.

4 Meanwhile, remove about 8 outer leaves of the cabbage and cut off any thick hard midribs. Bring another pan of salted water to the boil and blanch the cabbage leaves for 4 minutes. Drain and set aside. Chop the remaining cabbage and reserve.

5 Melt the margarine in a large saucepan, add the onion and fry gently for 5 minutes until soft.

6 Add the chopped cabbage to the pan and cook over moderate heat, stirring, for 5 minutes. Peel, core and chop the apple and add to the pan. Cook for a further minute.

7 Drain the rice thoroughly and add to the pan with the dates, orange zest

Sunflower seed peppers

SERVES 4

2 large green peppers, halved lengthways and deseeded

2 tablespoons sunflower oil

1 large onion, chopped

1 red pepper, deseeded and cut into 1 cm/ ½ inch squares

500 g/1 lb tomatoes, skinned and chopped

100 g/4 oz button mushrooms, quartered

50 g/2 oz sunflower seeds, toasted

½ teaspoon dried thyme

¼ teaspoon sweet paprika

salt and freshly ground black pepper

40 g/1½ oz Edam or Gouda cheese, roughly grated

1 Heat the oil in a medium saucepan, add the onion and fry gently for 5 minutes until soft and lightly col oured. Add the red pepper and fry for a further 2 minutes, stirring. Add the tomatoes, mushrooms, toasted sunflower seeds, thyme, paprika and salt and pepper to taste, then cook over a moderate heat for 10 minutes, stirring

Far left: Stuffed cabbage pie
Below: Sunflower seed peppers

constantly until the mixture is thick.

2 Meanwhile, bring a saucepan of salted water to the boil. Put in the green pepper halves, bring back to the boil and simmer for 6 minutes until just tender. Drain thoroughly.

3 Heat the grill to high. Put the green pepper halves on the grill rack and season them inside with salt and pepper. Pile the sunflower seed mixture into the pepper halves, pressing it down with a spoon. Sprinkle the cheese lightly on top.

4 Grill for a few minutes, until the cheese is melted. Serve at once.

Stuffed aubergines

SERVES 4

2 large aubergines

salt

4 tablespoons olive oil

2 onions, chopped

2 cloves garlic, crushed

500 g/1 lb tomatoes, skinned and chopped

freshly ground black pepper

1 teaspoon dried basil

3 tablespoons chopped fresh parsley

1 tablespoon lemon juice

chopped fresh parsley, to garnish

1 Trim the aubergines, halve them lengthways and scoop out the flesh, leaving a shell about 5 mm/¼ inch thick. Sprinkle the insides of the shells thickly with salt and leave them in a colander to drain. Chop the scooped out flesh coarsely, add to the colander and sprinkle with salt too. Leave to drain for about 1 hour.

2 Rinse the salt off the aubergines and dry the chopped flesh and the shells on absorbent paper. Heat the oven to 180C/350F/Gas 4.

3 Heat 2 tablespoons oil in a frying-pan, add the onion and garlic and cook for about 10 minutes, until the onion is soft. Add the chopped aubergine flesh and the tomatoes, with any juice they may have made. Season the mixture well and cook gently for about 15 minutes, until the aubergine is soft. Stir in the basil and chopped parsley and remove from the heat.

4 Put the aubergine shells in an ovenproof dish and spoon the cooked mixture into them.

5 Sprinkle the remaining olive oil and the lemon juice over the filling and bake for about 1 hour, until the flesh on the shells is tender.

6 Remove the aubergines from the oven and allow to cool, then refrigerate for about 1 hour before serving. Garnish the tops with chopped parsley.

Cheesy cornmeal pie

SERVES 4

175 g/6 oz cornmeal
salt and freshly ground black pepper
3 tablespoons vegetable oil
150 ml/¼ pint hot water
1 large onion, chopped
3 celery stalks, chopped
1 tablespoon tomato purée
100 g/4 oz Cheddar cheese, grated
4 tomatoes, skinned and sliced
6-8 stuffed olives sliced
melted margarine, for greasing

1 Heat the oven to 180C/350F/Gas 4. Grease the base and sides of a 22-23 cm/8½-9 inch loose-based flan tin.
2 Place the cornmeal, pinch of salt and 2 tablespoons vegetable oil in a bowl and pour on the hot water. Stir well, then mix with your fingers to form a smooth, soft dough.
3 Line the prepared flan tin with the warm dough, gently kneading it into place with your fingers. Set aside to cool.
4 Heat the remaining oil in a frying-pan. Add the onion and fry gently for 5 minutes until soft and lightly coloured. Add the celery and cook gently for another 10 minutes, stirring occa-

sionally. Stir in the tomato purée and season to taste with salt and freshly ground black pepper.
5 Sprinkle about one-third of the cheese evenly over the cornmeal base, then add the onion and celery mixture. Top with another third of the cheese. Arrange the sliced tomatoes on top, then sprinkle over the remaining cheese. Bake in the oven for about 35 minutes until the cheese topping is golden brown.
6 Remove the flan from the oven, arrange the sliced olives decoratively on top, then return to the oven for a further 5 minutes. Remove from tin and serve hot.

Swiss cheese fondue

SERVES 6

350 g/12 oz Gruyère cheese, coarsely grated
350 g/12 oz Emmental cheese, coarsely grated
1 clove garlic, halved
2 teaspoons cornflour
2 teaspoons kirsch
425 ml/³⁄₄ pint dry white wine
2 teaspoons lemon juice
pinch of white pepper
freshly grated nutmeg

To serve

1 large crusty French loaf, cut into 2.5 cm/
* 1 inch cubes*
cocktail onions
pickled gherkins

1 Rub round the inside of a fondue pot with the cut sides of the garlic. Put the cornflour in a small bowl and blend in the kirsch until smooth.
2 Pour the wine and lemon juice into the fondue pot, place over a moderate heat and bring almost to boiling point.
3 Remove from the heat and then gradually stir in the grated cheese.
4 Add the kirsch mixture, together

Left: Swiss cheese fondue
Below: Cheese and chive soufflé

with the pepper and a sprinkling of nutmeg, stirring constantly until smooth. (If the mixture seems too thick, add a little more warmed white wine and stir well to mix.)
5 Carefully transfer the pot to its burner and stand. To serve: guests spear a cube of bread on to a fondue fork and dip it into the hot fondue. Serve with onions and gherkins.
● Use an earthenware or enamelled iron fondue pot. If using a stainless steel fondue pot, make sure it has a thick base, as cheese is inclined to catch and burn if not watched.

Cheese and chive soufflé

SERVES 4

150 g/5 oz Cheddar cheese, finely grated
50 g/2 oz margarine or butter
1 small onion, finely chopped
40 g/1¹⁄₂ oz plain flour
pinch of mustard powder
pinch of cayenne pepper
300 ml/¹⁄₂ pint milk
4 large eggs, separated
1 tablespoon snipped chives
salt and freshly ground black pepper
melted margarine, for greasing

1 Brush the inside of a 1 L/2 pint soufflé dish with melted margarine. Heat the oven to 180C/350F/Gas 4.
2 Melt the margarine in a saucepan, add the onion and cook gently for about 5 minutes until soft and lightly coloured but not browned.
3 Sprinkle the flour, mustard and cayenne into the pan and stir over low heat for 2 minutes.
4 Remove from the heat and gradually stir in the milk. Return to the heat and simmer, stirring, until thick and smooth.
5 Remove the pan from heat, stir in the cheese, then leave the sauce to cool slightly. Beat the egg yolks, then stir them into the cheese sauce with the chives. Season well with pepper, and salt if necessary.
6 Whisk the egg whites until stiff but not dry. Fold them into the cheese mixture with a large metal spoon, in a figure-of-eight motion, using the edges of the spoon to cut through the mixture cleanly.
7 Pour the mixture into the prepared soufflé dish. Run a round-bladed knife through the mixture to make an attractive 'crown' effect.
8 Bake in the oven for 50 minutes or until the soufflé is well risen and golden. When lightly shaken, it should only wobble slightly. Serve at once straight from the dish.

Tasty cheese cakes

MAKES 8

100 g/4 oz Red Leicester or Cheshire cheese, coarsely grated

100 g/4 oz mature Cheddar cheese, finely grated

25 g/1 oz margarine or butter

1 small onion, very finely chopped

150 g/5 oz fresh wholemeal or white breadcrumbs

1/2 teaspoon dried thyme

100 g/4 oz cottage cheese

salt and freshly ground black pepper

2 eggs, beaten

1 teaspoon water

2 tablespoons chopped fresh parsley

vegetable oil, for frying

To garnish

8 small gherkins, halved or cut into fans

8 olives, stuffed with pimiento, halved

1 Melt the margarine in a frying-pan. Add the onion and fry gently for

---

Below: Egg and onion bake
Above right: Curried eggs with biriani rice

5 minutes until soft and lightly coloured. Remove from the pan with a slotted spoon; cool on absorbent paper.
2 In a bowl, mix the grated cheeses with 75 g/3 oz of the breadcrumbs, the thyme, cottage cheese, and salt and pepper to taste. Add two-thirds of the egg and mix throroughly.
3 Divide the mixture into 8 and shape each portion into a flat round cake. Refrigerate for 30 minutes – this will help them to hold their shape while they are cooking.
4 Mix the remaining egg with 1 teaspoon of cold water in a shallow bowl. Mix the remaining breadcrumbs with the parsley and salt and pepper; spread out on a flat plate.
5 Coat the cakes in the egg, then in the breadcrumb mixture
6 Heat about 1 cm/1/2 inch of oil in a frying-pan until it is hot enough to turn a stale bread cube golden in 50 seconds. Add the cakes to the pan and fry for 2-3 minutes on each side until just browned. Do not fry the cheese cakes longer than it takes to brown the outside or the cheese will melt too much. Drain well on absorbent paper.
7 Serve at once, garnished with gherkin and olive halves.

Egg and onion bake

SERVES 4

4 eggs

2 large onions, finely chopped

salt and freshly ground black pepper

600 ml/1 pint hot milk

75 g/3 oz Cheddar cheese, grated

15 g/1/2 oz butter

1 tablespoon sunflower or vegetable oil

2 tablespoons finely chopped fresh chervil or parsley

margarine, for greasing

Cheese sauce

25 g/1 oz butter

25 g/1 oz wholemeal or plain flour

300 ml/1/2 pint milk

100 g/4 oz Cheddar cheese, finely grated

1 teaspoon French mustard

1 Heat the oven to 150C/300F/Gas 2 and grease a 1 L/2 pint ovenproof dish with margarine.
2 Put the eggs in a bowl and season with salt and pepper. Whisk the eggs, then whisk in the milk and cheese and pour into the prepared dish. Half-fill a roasting tin with boiling water and

place the dish in the tin. Bake in the oven for 1½ hours or until the mixture is firm.

3 About 15 minutes before the end of the cooking time, heat the butter and oil in a frying-pan. Add the onions and fry gently for 5 minutes until soft and lightly coloured. Stir in the chervil, remove from the heat and set aside.

4 Heat the grill to high.

5 Meanwhile, make cheese sauce; melt the butter in a small saucepan, sprinkle in the flour and stir over low heat for 1-2 minutes until straw-coloured. Remove from the heat and gradually stir in the milk. Return to the heat and simmer, stirring, until thick and smooth. Stir in half the grated cheese and the mustard. Season to taste with salt and pepper.

6 When the egg mixture is cooked, spoon the fried onion mixture evenly over top.

7 Spoon the sauce over the layer of onions and sprinkle with the remaining cheese.

8 Place the dish under the grill until the cheese has melted and is golden brown and bubbling. Serve at once, straight from the dish.

Curried eggs with biriani rice

SERVES 4

8 eggs

2 tablespoons vegetable oil

1 onion, finely chopped

1 clove garlic, crushed

1 tablespoon ground cumin or coriander

1 teaspoon ground turmeric

½ teaspoon chilli powder or to taste

salt

4 large tomatoes, skinned and chopped

600 ml/1 pint vegetable stock

freshly ground black pepper

Biriani rice

225 g/8 oz basmati, patna or long-grain rice, rinsed and drained

2 tablespoon vegetable oil

1 teaspoon ground cumin

½ teaspoon ground turmeric

750 ml/1¼ pints vegetable stock

250 g/9 oz frozen mixed vegetables

25 g/1 oz softened butter

1 Cook the eggs in boiling water for 8 minutes until just hard-boiled. Drain and reserve.

2 Heat the oil in a large heavy-based pan or flameproof casserole, add the onion, garlic, spices and salt to taste and fry gently for 5 minutes until the onion is soft, stirring constantly.

3 Add the chopped tomatoes to the pan and stir-fry for a few minutes. Stir in the stock and bring to the boil. Lower the heat and simmer uncovered for 20 minutes, stirring occasionally.

4 Make the biriani rice: heat the oil in a heavy pan, add the rice, spices and salt to taste and fry gently for 5 minutes, stirring constantly.

5 Pour in the second quantity of stock and the frozen mixed vegetables, stir once, then cover and cook over gentle heat for 20 minutes until the rice is tender.

6 Shell the hard-boiled eggs and add to the curry sauce. Cook gently for a further 20 minutes, spooning the sauce over the eggs from time to time so they become well-coated.

7 When the rice is tender, fork in the softened butter and add salt and pepper to taste. Arrange the rice around the edge of a warmed serving dish.

8 Taste and adjust the seasoning of the sauce. Spoon the eggs into the centre of the rice, then pour the curry sauce over the top. Serve at once.

Lentil lasagne

SERVES 4-6

250 g/9 oz split red lentils
2 tablespoons vegetable oil, plus 1 teaspoon
1 onion, chopped
2 cloves garlic, crushed
1 small green pepper, deseeded and chopped
400 g/14 oz can tomatoes
1 bay leaf
400 ml/14 fl oz vegetable stock or water
150 ml/¼ pint red wine
2 tablespoons tomato ketchup
pinch each of dried oregano, thyme and basil
salt and freshly ground black pepper
125 g/4 oz dried wholewheat lasagne
1½ quantity cheese sauce (page 62)
50 g/2 oz Cheddar cheese, grated

1 Heat the oven to 200C/400F/Gas 6.
2 Heat 2 tablespoons oil in a saucepan, add the onion and fry gently for 10 minutes. Add the garlic, lentils, pepper, tomatoes, bay leaf, stock and wine. Bring to the boil and simmer gently for 45 minutes, until the lentils are tender. Remove the bay leaf, add the tomato ketchup and herbs, and season to taste with salt and pepper.
3 Meanwhile, cook the lasagne in a very large pan of salted water, with 1 teaspoon oil added to it, for about 12 minutes or until just tender. Drain, rinse under cold running water, then leave to drain on absorbent paper.
4 Put a layer of the lentil mixture into a shallow ovenproof dish and cover with some pieces of lasagne; follow this with another layer of the lentil mixture, then more lasagne and any remaining lentil mixture. Pour the cheese sauce over the top and sprinkle with the grated cheese.
5 Bake in the oven for about 45 minutes, until golden brown and bubbling.

Tagliatelle in parsley sauce

SERVES 4

350 g/12 oz fresh or dried tagliatelle
1 tablespoon vegetable oil
grated Parmesan cheese, to serve

Sauce
100 g/4 oz fresh parsley sprigs
2 large cloves garlic, chopped
25 g/1 oz pine kernels
150 ml/¼ pint olive oil
salt
50 g/2 oz Parmesan cheese, grated
freshly ground black pepper

1 First make the sauce: put the parsley, garlic, pine kernels and oil into a blender. Add a pinch of salt and blend the mixture for 1 minute until smooth.
2 Add all of the grated Parmesan cheese and purée for 1 minute more, then season with freshly ground black pepper to taste.
3 Bring a large pan of salted water to the boil. Add the oil and fresh tagliatelle and stir once. Bring back to the boil and cook for 2-3 minutes until tender, yet firm to the bite. (Cook dried tagliatelle for 10-12 minutes or according to packet instructions until tender.)

Below: Tagliatelle in parsley sauce
Far right: Creamy rigatoni

4 Drain the tagliatelle well, then turn into a warmed serving dish. Stir the sauce and add to the dish. Quickly toss the tagliatelle with 2 forks to mix it with the sauce.

5 Serve at once while still hot, with a bowl of Parmesan handed separately.

Creamy rigatoni

SERVES 4

350 g/12 oz dried rigatoni or short-cut
  macaroni

salt

1 tablespoon vegetable oil

150 g/5 oz butter

100 g/4 oz button mushrooms, sliced

150 ml/¼ pint single cream

2 egg yolks

75g/3 oz Parmesan cheese, grated

pinch of freshly grated nutmeg

freshly ground black pepper

100 g/4 oz frozen peas, cooked

50 g/2 oz Parmesan cheese, grated, to serve

1 Bring a large saucepan of salted water to the boil. Add the rigatoni and oil, lower the heat and simmer for about 12 minutes until tender, yet firm to the bite.

2 Meanwhile, melt 25 g/1 oz butter in a frying-pan. Add the mushrooms and fry over moderate heat until just tender. Set aside.

3 Make the sauce: melt the remaining butter in a large saucepan. Remove from the heat and set aside. In a bowl, quickly mix the cream, egg yolks and Parmesan with the nutmeg. Season with salt and plenty of pepper. Add this mixture to the melted butter in the pan and stir well.

4 When the rigatoni is nearly cooked, set the saucepan with the sauce mixture over very low heat to warm it through slightly: make sure that the eggs do not scramble.

5 Drain the cooked rigatoni, add to the cream sauce with the peas and the mushrooms. Stir continuously for a few seconds, then pile into warmed individual serving dishes, sprinkle with Parmesan and serve at once.

Pasta with tomatoes

SERVES 4

350 g/12 oz dried wholewheat
  spaghetti

grated Parmesan cheese, to serve

Sauce

25 g/1 oz butter

2 tablespoons olive or vegetable oil

2 onions, roughly chopped

1 clove garlic, crushed

750 g/1½ lb tomatoes, skinned and roughly
  chopped

225 ml/8 fl oz vegetable stock

65 g/2½ oz currants

2 teaspoons wine vinegar

1 teaspoon sugar

1 bay leaf

½ teaspoon dried basil

½ teaspoon dried thyme

¼ teaspoon ground cinnamon

salt and freshly ground black pepper

1 Make the sauce: heat the butter and oil in a large saucepan, add the onions and garlic and fry gently for 5 minutes until the onion is soft and lightly coloured

2 Add the tomatoes, stock, currants, vinegar, sugar, herbs and cinnamon. Season with salt and pepper. Bring to the boil then lower the heat and simmer, uncovered, for 40-50 minutes, until thick, stirring occasionally and breaking up the tomato pieces with a wooden spoon.

3 Bring a large pan of salted water to the boil and cook the spaghetti for 15-20 minutes or until tender, yet firm to the bite. Drain the spaghetti thoroughly in a colander.

4 Divide the spaghetti between 4 warmed individual serving plates or shallow soup bowls and top each with a ladleful of the hot sauce. Serve the spaghetti at once, with grated Parmesan cheese handed separately in a small bowl.

Aubergine pasta bake

SERVES 4

1 large aubergine

salt

4 tablespoons olive oil

1 clove garlic, crushed (optional)

1 onion, chopped

1 green or red pepper, deseeded and finely chopped

2 x 500 g/16 oz can tomatoes, chopped

75 ml/3 fl oz red wine

2 teaspoons tomato purée

½ teaspoon sugar

1 tablespoon finely chopped fresh basil or 1 teaspoon dried basil

freshly ground black pepper

175 g/6 oz dried tagliatelle

12 slices processed cheese

25 g/1 oz Parmesan cheese, grated

vegetable oil, for greasing

coriander sprigs, to garnish (optional)

1 Wipe the aubergine with a damp cloth and trim off the stalk. Slice the aubergine into 5 mm/¼ inch thick slices and put them in a colander in layers, sprinkling salt between each layer. Cover with a plate and place a heavy weight on top. Leave for about 1 hour to draw out the bitter juices then rinse the slices and pat dry on absorbent paper.

2 Heat the oven to 180C/350F/Gas 4.

3 Heat 1 tablespoon of the oil in a saucepan, add the garlic, if using, the onion and green pepper and fry gently for about 5 minutes until the onion is soft and lightly coloured. Stir in tomatoes with juices, wine and tomato purée. Bring to boil, stir in the sugar and basil and season with salt and pepper to taste. Let the sauce boil gently to reduce and thicken.

4 Meanwhile, bring a pan of salted water to the boil and add 1 teaspoon of oil. Cook the tagliatelle for 5-6 minutes until tender, yet firm to the bite, then drain thoroughly.

5 Heat the remaining oil in a frying-pan, add the aubergine slices and fry gently until they are lightly coloured on both sides. Remove with a slotted spoon and drain well on absorbent paper.

6 Grease an ovenproof dish with vegetable oil and spread a third of tomato sauce over the bottom. Put half the noodles on top, followed by half the aubergine slices and half the processed cheese. Cover with another third of the tomato sauce and then the remaining noodles, aubergine slices and processed cheese. Spread the remaining tomato sauce over the cheese slices and sprinkle the Parmesan cheese on top.

7 Cook the pasta bake in the oven for about 20 minutes, until heated through.

8 Garnish with coriander sprigs, if liked, and serve immediately straight from the dish.

Vegetable lasagne

SERVES 4

200 g/7 oz pre-cooked lasagne

2 tablespoons vegetable oil

1 onion, finely chopped

100 g/4 oz button mushrooms, sliced

250 g/9 oz frozen spinach, defrosted and well drained

1-2 tablespoons lemon juice

¼ teaspoon freshly grated nutmeg

salt and freshly ground black pepper

225 g/8 oz cottage cheese

100 g/4 oz mature Cheddar cheese, finely grated

275 g/10 oz can artichoke hearts, drained and finely chopped

margarine, for greasing

Sauce

25 g/1 oz margarine or butter

15 g/½ oz wholemeal or plain flour

225 ml/8 fl oz milk

4-5 tablespoons grated Parmesan cheese

1 Heat the oven to 190C/375F/Gas 5. Grease a 19-20 cm/7½-8 inch square, shallow ovenproof dish.

2 Heat the oil in a heavy-based pan and fry the onion for 3-4 minutes, until soft but not coloured. Add the mushrooms and cook, stirring, for 5 minutes. Add the spinach, lemon juice and nutmeg and season with salt and pepper. Simmer for 5-6 minutes, stirring occasionally.

3 Meanwhile, mix the cottage cheese with the grated Cheddar in a bowl; season to taste with pepper.

4 Make the sauce: melt margarine in a small pan, sprinkle in the flour and stir over a low heat for 1-2 minutes, until straw-coloured. Remove from heat and gradually stir in the milk. Return to the heat and simmer, stirring, until thick and smooth. Add the Parmesan cheese and salt and pepper to taste.

5 Put one-third of the lasagne in the prepared dish, spread with half the cottage cheese mixture, then the spinach mixture. Top with another third of lasagne, spread with the remaining cottage cheese mixture, then the artichoke hearts. Cover with the remaining lasagne and spread sauce on top.

6 Bake in oven for 30-35 minutes, until the top is bubbling and golden. Leave to cool slightly before serving.

Spaghetti with courgette sauce

SERVES 4

350 g/12 oz dried wholewheat spaghetti

2 tablespoons vegetable oil

50 g/2 oz butter

1 onion, finely chopped

1 clove garlic, finely chopped

1 green pepper, deseeded and thinly sliced

500 g/1 lb courgettes, trimmed and cut into 5 mm/¼ inch slices

350 g/12 oz tomatoes, skinned, deseeded and sliced

1 teaspoon dried oregano

salt and freshly ground black pepper

grated Parmesan cheese, to serve

1 To make the sauce: heat the oil and 25 g/1 oz butter in a frying-pan, add the onion and fry gently for 5 minutes until soft and lightly coloured. Add the garlic, green pepper and courgettes, stir well and fry over moderate heat for 2 minutes. Cover the pan, lower the heat and simmer for 10 minutes, stirring occasionally.

2 Add the tomatoes and oregano, with the salt and pepper to taste, and cook, uncovered, over moderate heat for a further 10 minutes. Taste the courgette sauce and adjust the seasoning if necessary.

3 Meanwhile, cook the spaghetti in a large pan of boiling, salted water for 15-20 minutes, or until just tender.

4 Drain the spaghetti and toss it with the remaining butter in a warmed serving dish. Top with the sauce and serve hot, with the cheese handed separately.

Pasta kugel

SERVES 4

200 g/7 oz dried wholewheat pasta rings

3 eggs

225 g/8 oz curd cheese

150 ml/¼ pint soured cream

2 tablespoons soft brown sugar

100 g/4 oz seedless raisins

¼ teaspoon salt

¼ teaspoon ground cinnamon

¼ teaspoon freshly grated nutmeg

margarine, for greasing

fresh peaches, to serve

Topping

2 tablespoons chopped mixed nuts

¼ teaspoon ground cinnamon

15 g/½ oz butter

1 Heat the oven to 180C/350F/Gas 4. Grease a 1 L/2 pint ovenproof dish generously with margarine.

Far left: Aubergine pasta bake
Above: Spaghetti with courgette sauce

2 Bring a pan of salted water to the boil and cook the pasta rings for 12 minutes or according to packet instructions until they are tender, but still firm to the bite.

3 Meanwhile, beat the eggs in a bowl, add the curd cheese, soured cream and sugar and beat with a fork until smooth. Mix in the raisins, salt and spices.

4 Drain the cooked pasta rings and return them to the rinsed-out pan. Pour the curd cheese mixture over the pasta and stir it until evenly coated. Transfer the mixture to the prepared dish, sprinkle with nuts and cinnamon and dot the surface with the butter.

5 Bake in the oven, uncovered, for about 30 minutes, until the top is golden and filling has set around the edge but is still creamy in the middle. Serve the baked pasta at once, straight from the dish accompanied by fresh sliced peaches.

● *Kugel* is the Jewish name for a pudding, usually made of noodles or potatoes and baked. Although many kugels, like this one, are semi-sweet, they are generally served as a savoury meal.

Salads

You'll find a salad for every occasion in this chapter – add colour and texture to a meal with a crunchy side salad, or keep healthy with a substantial salad for lunch or supper.

Gado-gado

SERVES 4

1 potato, scrubbed but unpeeled
100 g/4 oz green cabbage or spring greens, shredded
100 g/4 oz French beans, sliced
100 g/4 oz carrots, thinly sliced
1/2 cauliflower, divided into florets
1 bunch of watercress, divided into sprigs
100 g/4 oz beansprouts
Sauce
100 g/4 oz shelled raw (not roasted or salted) peanuts
vegetable oil, for frying
1 clove garlic, crushed
2 shallots or 1/2 small onion, finely chopped
salt
1/2 teaspoon chilli powder
1/2 teaspoon light soft brown sugar
350 ml/12 fl oz water
juice of 1 lemon
To garnish
1 large egg, hard-boiled and cut into wedges
1 lettuce, shredded
1/4 cucumber, sliced
1 onion, sliced into rings and fried until crisp and brown
crackers or crisps

1 Make the sauce: heat enough oil in a large, heavy frying-pan or wok to cover the peanuts. Add the peanuts and fry over moderate heat for 5-6 minutes, stirring occasionally. Remove the peanuts with a slotted spoon and drain on absorbent paper. Leave to cool. Pour all but 1 teaspoon of the oil out of the pan.
2 Grind the cooled peanuts to a fine powder in a food processor or coffee grinder, or pound them to a fine powder, using a pestle and mortar.
3 Reheat the oil in the pan, add the garlic and shallots, season with salt and fry for 1 minute. Stir in the chilli powder and sugar and add the water. Bring the mixture to the boil, then stir in the ground peanuts. Lower the heat and simmer, stirring occasionally, for 4-6 minutes until the sauce thickens. Set aside.
4 Bring 3 saucepans of salted water to the boil. Add the potato to 1 pan and boil gently for 15 minutes.
5 Meanwhile, add the cabbage, French beans, carrots and cauliflower to another pan and boil gently for 4 minutes.
6 Add the watercress and beansprouts to the third pan and boil gently for 2-3 minutes.
7 Drain all the vegetables very thoroughly. Allow the potato to cool slightly, then cut into thin slices.
8 Pile the warm cabbage, French beans, carrots, cauliflower, watercress and beansprouts on to a round serving dish. Arrange the potato slices and hard-boiled egg wedges on top, and arrange the shredded lettuce and sliced cucumber round the edge.
9 Stir the lemon juice into the sauce in the pan and heat through gently. Pour the sauce over the salad. Garnish with fried onion rings and crackers, broken up. Serve at once.

● This popular Indonesian salad is best served with the vegetables still just warm. Peanuts feature prominently in Indonesian cooking, and Gado-gado – which means 'a mixture' – is topped with a nutty sauce. Make sure that you buy raw peanuts: roasted or salted ones will not give the right flavour or texture.

Bulgur wheat and parsley salad

SERVES 4

225 g/8 oz bulgur wheat
1.25 L/2 pints warm water
175 g/6 oz fresh parsley, chopped
4 spring onions, finely chopped
6 tablespoons olive oil
juice of 1 lemon
1 clove garlic, crushed
salt and freshly ground black pepper
250 g/9 oz tomatoes, cut in wedges
4 thin lemon slices, to garnish

1 Put the bulgur wheat into a large bowl. Pour in the water and leave to soak for 45 minutes. Drain the wheat in a sieve and using your hands, squeeze out as much water as possible. Put the drained wheat into a large bowl.
2 Mix the chopped parsley and spring onions into the wheat.
3 Beat together the oil, lemon juice, garlic and plenty of salt and pepper. Fold the dressing into the wheat and parsley mixture.
4 Pile the salad on to a flat serving dish, building it up into a pyramid. Arrange the tomato wedges around the edge of the dish.
5 To make lemon twists for garnish: make a cut from the outside of one lemon slice to the centre, then twist one half of the slice backwards. Repeat with remaining slices. Place the lemon twists on top of the salad. Serve at room temperature.

Gado-Gado, an attractive salad made from lightly cooked vegetables

Chick-pea salad

SERVES 4

100 g/4 oz chick-peas
3 tablespoons olive oil
1 tablespoon wine vinegar
salt and freshly ground black pepper
500 g/1 lb tomatoes, skinned and sliced
1 onion, thinly sliced
2 teaspoons chopped fresh basil, or 1 teaspoon dried basil

1 Put the chick-peas into a deep bowl, cover with plenty of cold water and leave to soak for 8 hours.
2 Drain the chick-peas, rinse under cold running water, then put them into a saucepan and cover with fresh cold water. Bring to the boil, then reduce heat and simmer for about 1 hour until tender. Add more water during cooking if necessary.
3 Drain the cooked chick-peas and leave to cool.
4 Put the oil and vinegar into a bowl. Mix together with a fork, and season to taste with salt and pepper. Add the chick-peas and mix gently until well coated with dressing. Take care not to break them up.
5 Lay the tomato and onion slices in a shallow serving dish and sprinkle with the basil and salt and pepper to taste. Spoon the dressed chick-peas over the top. Serve cold.

Brown rice salad

SERVES 4

150 g/5 oz brown rice
salt
1 red pepper, deseeded and diced
1 green pepper, deseeded and diced
25 g/1 oz margarine or butter
1 Spanish onion, chopped
250 g/9 oz tomatoes, skinned, deseeded and chopped
1/2 small cucumber, diced
halved stuffed olives and bunch of watercress, to garnish

Dressing

3 tablespoons vegetable oil
1 teaspoon wine vinegar or lemon juice
pinch of mustard powder
pinch of caster sugar
salt and freshly ground black pepper

1 Rinse the rice and put it into a large saucepan of boiling salted water. Bring to the boil again, reduce heat and simmer, very gently, for about 40 minutes, until the rice is cooked and has absorbed all the water. If necessary, add more boiling water during cooking. Rinse under cold running water and leave in a sieve to drain.
2 Meanwhile, soften the diced peppers slightly by plunging them into boiling water for 30 seconds. Drain and refresh immediately under cold running water.

3 Melt the margarine in a frying-pan, add the onion and cook over gentle heat for 5 minutes until it is soft and translucent. Remove from the heat and stir in the peppers, tomatoes and cucumber.
4 Put the ingredients for the dressing in a large bowl and whisk with a fork to blend thoroughly.
5 Add the drained rice to the dressing with the vegetables and gently mix all the ingredients together, using 2 forks. Pack into a 850 ml/1½ pint plain ring mould and refrigerate for at least 1 hour.
6 To unmould: run a knife around the ring mould. Invert a serving plate on top and give the mould a sharp tap. Fill the centre of the ring with watercress and surround with halved olives. Serve at once.

Stuffed cucumber salad

SERVES 4

1 large cucumber, cut into 24 even slices
1 round lettuce, leaves separated
350 g/12 oz carrots, finely grated
3 tablespoons sultanas
small parsley sprigs and a few chopped walnuts, to garnish

Filling

250 g/9 oz curd cheese
75 g/3 oz shelled walnuts, chopped
2 teaspoons finely chopped fresh parsley
2 teaspoons snipped chives or finely chopped spring onion
½ teaspoon sweet paprika
salt and freshly ground black pepper.

Dressing

5 tablespoons vegetable oil
2 tablespoons white wine or cider vinegar
large pinch of mustard powder
pinch of caster sugar

1 Make the filling: put all the filling ingredients in a bowl, season with salt and pepper and mix well.
2 Remove the seeds from each slice of cucumber with an apple corer or a small sharp knife. Season with salt and pepper and set out on a flat plate.
3 Divide the filling between the cucumber slices, pressing it into the central hole and piling it up on top.
4 Make the dressing: put all the dressing ingredients in a screw-top jar, season with salt and pepper, then shake the jar well to mix.
5 Arrange the lettuce leaves on 4 individual plates and drizzle a teaspoonful of the dressing over each serving. Transfer 6 cucumber slices to each plate, arranging them in a ring.
6 Mix the grated carrots with the sultanas in a bowl and add the remaining dressing. Toss to coat thoroughly, then pile into the centre of the rings of stuffed cucumber slices. Garnish 3 cucumber slices on each plate with a parsley sprig and 3 slices with a few chopped walnuts. Serve at once.

Above left: Brown rice salad
Right: Gazpacho salad

Gazpacho salad

SERVES 4

1 red pepper, deseeded and thinly sliced
1 green pepper, deseeded and thinly sliced
½ large cucumber, peeled and thinly sliced
350 g/12 oz tomatoes, skinned and thinly sliced
sugar, for sprinkling
1 onion, thinly sliced
salt and freshly ground black pepper
10 tablespoons fresh white or wholemeal breadcrumbs

French dressing

6 tablespoons olive oil
2 tablespoons lemon juice
1 clove garlic, crushed

To serve

10 black olives
1 tablespoon chopped fresh parsley

1 Plunge the peppers in boiling water for 30 seconds, and then immerse them immediately in cold water.
2 Make the French dressing: put all the ingredients in a screw-top jar, season with salt and pepper, then shake the jar well to mix well.
3 In a glass bowl, put a layer of cucumber, followed by a layer of tomatoes and a sprinkling of sugar, a layer of onion and a layer of mixed red and green peppers. Season with salt and pepper and sprinkle over 2 tablespoons breadcrumbs and 2 tablespoons French dressing.
4 Continue these layers, finishing with a layer of 4 tablespoons breadcrumbs. Cover these with French dressing so that they are well soaked, then cover the bowl with cling film and refrigerate for 2-3 hours.
5 Just before serving, sprinkle with olives and chopped parsley.

Wheaty pea and vegetable salad

SERVES 4

100 g/4 oz wholewheat grains

100 g/4 oz green or yellow split peas

2 tablespoons olive oil

1 tablespoon red wine vinegar

salt and freshly ground black pepper

2 carrots, grated

2 celery stalks, chopped

5 cm/2 inch piece of cucumber, peeled and chopped

4 spring onions, chopped

2 tomatoes, skinned and chopped

4 lettuce leaves, shredded

2 tablespoons raisins

a little cress, to garnish

Dressing

175 g/6 oz curd cheese

4 tablespoons milk

1 tablespoon thick bottled mayonnaise

1 Put the wholewheat grains in a bowl, cover with cold water and leave to soak for 8 hours or overnight.

2 Next day, cook the wholewheat grains in a pressure cooker for 25 minutes, or simmer in plenty of water for 1¼ – 1½ hours, or until the grains are tender and beginning to burst. Drain and cool slightly.

3 Meanwhile, put the split peas into a saucepan of cold water and simmer for about 25 minutes, until just tender but still whole.

4 Put the oil and vinegar into a large bowl and mix together. Season with salt and pepper to taste, then add the wheat and peas. Leave until cold.

5 Stir in the carrots, celery, cucumber, spring onions, tomatoes, lettuce and raisins, tossing gently until well coated with the oil and vinegar mixture. Divide the salad between 4 individual bowls.

6 Make the dressing: beat together the curd cheese, milk and mayonnaise until smooth.

7 Put a large spoonful of dressing on top of each bowl of salad and sprinkle with cress. Serve at once.

Two-bean salad

SERVES 4

100 g/4 oz dried red kidney beans, soaked overnight

100 g/4 oz dried haricot beans, soaked overnight

1 small onion, chopped

1 bay leaf

2 large celery stalks, thinly sliced

1 green pepper, deseeded and diced

Dressing

6 tablespoons olive oil

2 tablespoons wine vinegar

1 clove garlic, crushed

½ teaspoon French mustard (optional)

salt and freshly ground black pepper

1 Drain the kidney beans and haricot beans. Transfer the beans to a saucepan, cover with water and bring to the boil. Boil vigorously for 10 minutes, to remove any toxins, then drain and cover with fresh water.

2 Add onion and bay leaf and bring back to the boil. Reduce the heat slightly, half cover with a lid and simmer for about 1 hour until the beans are tender.

3 Meanwhile, make the dressing: put the ingredients in a screw-top jar, with salt and pepper to taste. Replace the lid firmly and shake well to mix the dressing.

4 Drain the beans and discard the cooking liquid and bay leaf. Transfer to a serving dish and pour over the dressing, while the beans are still warm. Mix well and leave to stand for at least 1 hour or overnight.

5 Add the celery and diced pepper to the beans, taste and adjust seasoning, if necessary, and stir to mix well. Serve at once.

White cabbage salad

SERVES 6

500 g/1 lb white cabbage
1/2 cucumber
6 spring onions
3 hard-boiled eggs, to garnish
Dressing
5 tablespoons vegetable oil
2 tablespoons white wine vinegar
2 tablespoons chopped fresh mint
1/4 teaspoon French mustard
salt and freshly ground black pepper

1 Remove the coarse stalk of the cabbage. Finely shred the cabbage and put into a salad bowl.

2 Cut the cucumber into small dice about 5 mm/1/4 inch square and add to the cabbage.

3 Thinly slice the spring onions and add to the salad.

4 Make the dressing: put the ingredients in a screw-top jar, with salt and pepper to taste. Replace the lid firmly and shake well to mix.

5 Cut the hard-boiled eggs into thin slices. Place the egg slices around the edge of the cabbage and cucumber salad. Pour over the dressing, toss until the salad is thoroughly coated and serve at once.

Above left: Two-bean salad makes a substantial side dish
Right: Serve White cabbage and cucumber salad for a light lunch

Sweet pepper salad

SERVES 6

4 peppers
1 Spanish onion, finely sliced
4 tablespoons olive oil
2 tablespoons white wine vinegar
salt

1 Heat the grill to high.
2 Wash the peppers and pat dry thoroughly with absorbent paper. Place the peppers on the grill rack and grill them, turning them often with kitchen tongs until the skins are charred black on all sides.

3 Immediately transfer the peppers to a large bowl and cover closely with several layers of absorbent paper to seal in the heat and allow the peppers to cook through. Cover the bowl tightly with a clean cloth; leave at room temperature for at least 24 hours.
4 The next day, remove the skins: one at a time, hold the peppers under cold running water and rub off the skins with your fingers. Gently squeezing the base of each pepper, pull out the core and the seeds in one piece. Discard the cores and seeds. Rinse peppers under cold running water.
5 Tear peppers into long strips with your fingers and arrange on a serving dish with the finely sliced onion.
6 Put the oil in a small bowl with the vinegar and salt to taste. Mix well with a fork, then pour over the peppers. Serve as soon as possible, at room temperature.

Beetroot and orange salad

SERVES 4

4 cooked beetroot, skinned and sliced
2 oranges
1 lettuce, leaves separated
2 large tomatoes, sliced
3-4 teaspoons chopped walnuts
Dressing
1 teaspoon finely chopped onion
1 teaspoon snipped chives
good pinch of salt
1/2 teaspoon English made mustard
good pinch of caster sugar
freshly ground black pepper
3 tablespoons olive or vegetable oil
1 tablespoon wine vinegar
dash of soy sauce

1 Peel the oranges over a bowl to catch the juices; reserve juice. Slice oranges.
2 Line a salad platter with lettuce. Arrange the orange and beetroot slices alternately in a ring on top of the lettuce. Arrange overlapping slices of tomato in the centre of the dish and sprinkle with walnuts.
3 Make the dressing: put all the ingredients in a screw-top jar with the reserved orange juice. Shake to mix well.
4 Spoon the dressing over the salad and serve at once.

Tangy potato salad

SERVES 6

500 g/1 lb potatoes, cut into even-sized chunks
salt
175 ml/6 fl oz thick bottled mayonnaise or soured cream
1 tablespoon olive oil
1 tablespoon grated fresh horseradish
freshly ground black pepper
1/2 teaspoon sweet paprika
1 teaspoon chopped fresh parsley

1 Put the potato chunks in a large saucepan; cover with cold water, add a pinch of salt and bring to the boil. Lower the heat slightly and simmer for 20-25 minutes until the potatoes are tender.

2 Meanwhile, put the mayonnaise into a large serving bowl and stir in the olive oil, horseradish and salt and pepper to taste.

3 Drain the potatoes and leave to cool slightly for about 10 minutes.

4 Add the potatoes to the mayonnaise, carefully turning them to ensure that all the pieces are evenly coated. Leave the potato salad to stand for 1 hour.

5 Just before serving, sprinkle over the paprika and parsley.

Watercress salad with curry dressing

SERVES 6

4 bunches of watercress, weighing about 500 g/1 lb in total

2 oranges

Dressing

6-8 tablespoons olive oil

2 tablespoons wine vinegar

1 tablespoon lemon juice

1 tablespoon curry powder

coarse salt and freshly ground black pepper

1 Rinse the watercress gently and remove the thick stem ends and any damaged or yellowed leaves. Drain well, then pat dry. Refrigerate for at least 1 hour.

2 Peel the oranges with a sharp, serrated knife; trim away the pith. Cut between the segments and the membranes to remove the orange segements. Remove any pips from the segments. Set aside.

3 Make the dressing: put all the ingredients in a bowl with salt and pepper to taste. Beat well to mix. Refrigerate until ready to assemble the salad.

4 To serve: place the watercress in a salad bowl and arrange the orange segments on top. Stir the dressing and pour over the salad. Toss the salad at the table, until each leaf of watercress is glistening with dressing.

Far left: Sweet pepper salad
Right: Greek-style mushrooms

Greek-style mushrooms

SERVES 4

500 g/1 lb small button mushrooms

5 tablespoons olive oil

1 onion, very finely chopped

6 tablespoons water

juice of ½ lemon

1 clove garlic, crushed

½ teaspoon dried thyme

2 bay leaves

250 g/9 oz tomatoes, skinned, deseeded and chopped

2 tablespoons chopped fresh parsley

salt and freshly ground black pepper

1 Heat half the oil in a saucepan, add the onion and cook over moderate heat for about 5 minutes, until soft and lightly coloured.

2 Add the water, lemon juice, garlic, thyme, bay leaves, tomatoes and half the parsley. Season with salt and pepper to taste. Bring to the boil, then lower the heat and simmer very gently for 3-4 minutes, stirring occasionally.

3 Add the mushrooms to the tomato sauce and simmer gently, uncovered, for 15 minutes.

4 Remove from the heat and discard the bay leaves.

5 Transfer the mixture to a serving dish. (If the sauce is too thin, transfer the mushrooms to a serving dish with a slotted spoon and boil the sauce for a few minutes to reduce.)

6 Garnish the mushroom dish with the remaining parsley and serve warm, cold or chilled.

Avocado and grapefruit salad

SERVES 4

2 small avocados

1 small grapefruit

2 dessert apples

1 small lettuce, leaves separated

Dressing

1 tablespoon clear honey

2 tablespoons cider vinegar

6 tablespoons olive oil

salt and freshly ground black pepper

1 To make the dressing: mix together the honey, vinegar and olive oil in a bowl. Whisk with a fork and season to taste.

2 Peel the grapefruit. Hold it over a bowl to catch the juice and, using a small, sharp knife, trim away any white pith. Divide the grapefruit into segments and stir into the dressing.

3 Just before serving, halve the avocados lengthways, then remove the stones and peel. Slice the flesh and add immediately to the dressing. Toss.

4 Quarter, core and slice the apples. Toss them in the dressing. Taste and adjust seasoning. Arrange the lettuce leaves in a salad bowl, pile the salad in the centre and serve at once.

Cucumber and strawberry salad

SERVES 4

1/2 cucumber, peeled and thinly sliced

100 g/4 oz strawberries, sliced lengthways

salt

sprigs of fennel leaves, to garnish

Above: Avocado and grapefruit salad
Far right: Oriental citrus salad

Dressing

1 tablespoon olive oil

1 tablespoon white wine vinegar

1 teaspoon caster sugar

freshly ground black pepper

1 Spread the cucumber out on a plate, sprinkle with salt and leave to stand for 30 minutes to draw out excess moisture. Drain and pat dry.

2 Make the dressing: put all the dressing ingredients in a screw-top jar with salt and pepper. Shake to mix.

3 Arrange alternate circles of cucumber and strawberries on a flat, round serving plate.

4 Spoon the dressing over the salad, garnish with sprigs of fennel leaves and serve the salad at once.

Plum salad

SERVES 4

175 g/6 oz dessert plums
1/4 cucumber, cut into matchsticks
1 round lettuce, shredded
6 spring onions, finely chopped
4 sage leaves, chopped
1 tablespoon chopped fresh tarragon
1 tablespoon chopped fresh parsley
4 tablespoons olive oil
2 tablespoons white wine vinegar
salt and freshly ground black pepper

1 Halve and stone the plums and cut them lengthways into thin slices.

2 Put the plum and cucumber slices, lettuce and spring onions in a salad bowl and mix in the herbs. Beat the oil with the vinegar, then season to taste with salt and pepper. Fold into the salad and serve at once.

Oriental citrus salad

SERVES 4

1 grapefruit
2 oranges
1/2 cucumber, sliced
1 onion, sliced into rings
225 g/8 oz can water chestnuts, drained and sliced
100 g/4 oz fresh spinach, washed and thoroughly dried
100 g/4 oz Edam cheese, sliced
1 tablespoon white wine vinegar
2 tablespoons sugar
2 teaspoons soy sauce
few drops of Tabasco

1 Peel the grapefruit and oranges and divide into segments, over a bowl to catch any juice. Put the fruit into a large bowl and mix in the cucumber, onion rings and the water chestnuts.

2 Arrange spinach on a serving platter, then place the cheese in overlapping slices at the edge.

3 Put the vinegar, sugar, soy sauce and Tabasco into the bowl with the collected fruit juices and whisk with a fork until well blended. Pour over the fruit mixture and toss.

4 Spoon the tossed salad on to the spinach. Refrigerate for 30 minutes, then serve at once.

Vegetable Accompaniments

With a little imagination, even the most familiar vegetables can be turned into exciting accompaniment dishes.

Chestnut sprouts

SERVES 4

500 g/1 lb small Brussels sprouts

salt

250 g/9 oz chestnuts

150 ml/¼ pint vegetable stock

1 celery stalk, halved

25 g/1 oz butter

pinch of freshly grated nutmeg

freshly ground black pepper

1 Wash the sprouts, cut off the stem ends and remove any discoloured leaves. Cut a cross in the stem end of each and leave to soak in a bowl of cold salted water.

2 Meanwhile, prepare the chestnuts: nick each with a sharp knife, then place in a saucepan and cover with cold water. Gradually bring to the boil and simmer for 10 minutes.

3 Remove the chestnuts from the heat, drain, then wrap in a thick folded tea-towel to keep hot: they must be kept hot to make peeling easier. Peel the chestnuts one at a time: hold in a soft cloth or oven glove, insert a small sharp knife into the slit in the skin and prise off the outer and inner skins.

4 Place the peeled chestnuts in a saucepan, cover with stock and add the celery. Bring to the boil, then lower the heat and simmer gently for 30-40 minutes or until the peeled chestnuts are tender.

5 Meanwhile, bring a pan of salted water to the boil. Drain the sprouts and add to the pan. Cover and simmer for 8-10 minutes until just tender. The sprouts should be just tender but still firm; they will have a nice 'nutty' texture and flavour. If overcooked they will be soft and will break up when combined with the chestnuts.

6 Drain the chestnuts and discard the celery. Drain the sprouts thoroughly, then return to the rinsed-out pan together with the chestnuts. Add the butter, nutmeg and salt and pepper to taste and toss to combine. Turn into a warmed serving dish and serve.

Sesame sprouts

SERVES 4

750 g/1½ lb Brussels sprouts

salt and freshly ground black pepper

50 g/2 oz margarine or butter

1 onion, finely chopped

1 clove garlic, crushed (optional)

25 g/1 oz plain flour

4 tablespoons tahini paste

½ vegetable stock cube, crumbled

350 ml/12 fl oz orange juice

150 ml/¼ pint water

1 teaspoon clear honey

2 teaspoons sesame seeds

orange twists, to garnish

1 Wash and trim the Brussels sprouts, discarding any tough or discoloured outer leaves. Cut a cross in stem end of each sprout.

2 Bring a pan of salted water to the boil and cook the Brussels sprouts for 8-10 minutes, until tender but still firm to the bite.

3 Meanwhile, make the sauce: melt the margarine in a small saucepan, add the onion and the garlic, if using, and fry gently for 5 minutes until the onion is soft and lightly coloured. Sprinkle in the flour and stir over low heat for 3 minutes. Add the tahini paste and crumbled stock cube and stir until smooth. Gradually stir in the orange juice and water, then simmer, stirring until thick and smooth. Stir in the honey and season to taste with salt and pepper.

4 Drain Brussels sprouts, transfer to a warmed serving dish and pour over the sauce. Sprinkle with sesame seeds, garnish with orange twists and serve at once.

Cauliflower creole

SERVES 4

1 cauliflower

1 tablespoon vegetable oil

1 large onion, chopped

1 clove garlic, crushed (optional)

400 g/14 oz can tomatoes

salt

25 g/1 oz margarine or butter

1 large green or red pepper, deseeded and chopped

½-1 teaspoon Tabasco

freshly ground black pepper

1 Heat the oil in a large saucepan, add the onion and garlic, if using, and fry for 2-3 minutes until just tender.

2 Stir in the tomatoes, breaking them up against the sides of the pan with a wooden spoon. Cover the saucepan and simmer gently for 20-30 minutes.

3 Meanwhile, bring a pan of salted water to the boil, plunge the cauliflower head down in it and cook for about 20 minutes until just tender. It is important not to overcook the cauliflower: it should feel quite firm when pierced with a knife.

4 Heat the oven to 130C/250F/Gas ½. Drain the cauliflower well, place on a warmed serving dish and keep hot in the oven.

5 Add the margarine and green pepper to the tomato sauce, stir well and simmer for 5 minutes. Season to taste with Tabasco, salt and freshly ground black pepper.

6 Pour a little of the sauce over the cauliflower, leaving some of the white flower showing. Pour the remaining sauce round the sides of the cauliflower. Serve at once.

Far left: Chestnut sprouts
Below: Cauliflower creole

Crunchy provençal beans

SERVES 4

350 g/12 oz frozen French beans
1 tablespoon vegetable oil
1 onion, chopped
1 large clove garlic, crushed
250 g/9 oz tomatoes, skinned and roughly chopped
1 teaspoon dried basil
salt and freshly ground black pepper
margarine, for greasing
tomato slices, to garnish

Topping

75 g/3 oz Cheddar cheese, grated
50 g/2 oz fresh wholemeal breadcrumbs

1 Heat the oven to 220C/425F/Gas 7. Grease an ovenproof dish.
2 Heat the oil in a heavy-based saucepan. Add the onion and garlic and fry gently for 10 minutes until the onion is soft and lightly coloured.
3 Add the tomatoes, with the basil and salt and pepper to taste, then simmer over moderate heat, uncovered, for 10 minutes, stirring occasionally.

4 Meanwhile, cook the beans in boiling salted water for 8 minutes until they are just tender. Drain.
5 Stir the beans into the tomato mixture, then taste and adjust seasoning. Transfer to the greased dish.
6 Mix the grated cheese with the breadcrumbs and sprinkle evenly over the bean mixture. Place in the oven for 15-20 minutes until the top has browned. Serve at once, garnished with tomato slices.

Below: French bean special
Far right: Orange potato croquettes

French bean special

SERVES 4

500 g/1 lb frozen French beans

salt

chopped fresh parsley, to garnish

Sauce

3 egg yolks

1 tablespoon white wine vinegar

small pinch of freshly grated nutmeg

1 teaspoon sugar (optional)

2 tablespoons double cream or soured cream

1 hard-boiled egg, finely chopped

freshly ground black pepper

1 Bring a large pan of salted water to the boil, add the beans and cook for 8 minutes or until the beans are just tender.

2 Meanwhile, make the sauce: put the egg yolks, vinegar, nutmeg and sugar, if using, into a heatproof bowl then stand the bowl over a pan of gently simmering water – make sure that the bottom of the bowl does not touch the water or the eggs will cook too quickly. Whisk over very low heat for about 6 minutes, or until thick enough to coat the back of a spoon.

3 Remove the pan from the heat and immediately beat in the cream and chopped hard-boiled egg. Season the mixture to taste with salt and freshly ground black pepper.

4 Drain the beans and turn them on to a warmed serving plate. Pour over the sauce and garnish with chopped parsley. Serve at once.

1 Shell the beans, then put them in a saucepan and pour over enough water to just cover them. Add the salt, cover the pan and bring to the boil, then lower the heat slightly and simmer for about 5 minutes until just tender.

2 Meanwhile, melt the butter in a frying-pan, add the crushed garlic and fry gently for 2 minutes. Remove the pan from the heat.

3 Drain the beans and add to the garlic in the frying-pan. Stir over moderate heat for 1 minute, then season to taste with salt and pepper and turn into a warmed serving dish. Serve at once, garnished with parsley.

Broad beans with garlic

SERVES 4-6

1 kg/2 lb fresh broad beans, unshelled weight

pinch of salt

25 g/1 oz butter

1 clove garlic, crushed

juice of ½ lemon

freshly ground black pepper

parsley sprigs, to garnish

Orange potato croquettes

SERVES 4

500 g/1 lb potatoes, boiled and drained well

1 egg yolk

15 g/½ oz margarine or butter

2 tablespoons hot milk

finely grated zest of 1 large orange

salt and freshly ground black pepper

vegetable oil, for deep-frying

orange slices, cut into twists, to garnish

Coating

1 egg, beaten

175 g/6 oz fine dried breadcrumbs

40 g/1½ oz plain flour

1 Put the hot drained potatoes in a saucepan, place over low heat and shake the pan vigorously until the potatoes are completely dry. Turn into a bowl, then mash.

2 Stir the egg yolk, margarine and hot milk into the mashed potato, beat until smooth. Beat in half the orange zest and season with salt and pepper to taste.

3 Divide the creamed potato into 16 portions. With floured hands, roll into cork shapes about 5 cm/2 inches long.

4 Put the beaten egg and breadcrumbs in separate shallow dishes. Stir the remaining orange zest into the breadcrumbs. Roll the potato croquettes in flour, then dip in beaten egg and roll in breadcrumbs.

5 Heat the oil in a deep-fat frier to 190C/375F or until a bread cube turns brown in 50 seconds. Lower the croquettes into the oil and fry for 4-5 minutes until golden brown. Remove with a slotted spoon and drain on absorbent paper. Serve hot, garnished with orange twists.

Scalloped potatoes

SERVES 4-6

750 g/1½ lb potatoes, thinly sliced

1 onion, chopped

100 g/4 oz Cheddar cheese, grated

salt and freshly ground black pepper

15 g/½ oz margarine or butter

1 egg

300 ml/½ pint milk

margarine, for greasing

1 Heat the oven to 180C/350F/Gas 4. Grease a shallow ovenproof dish.

2 Arrange a layer of potato slices in the dish and sprinkle with a little of the onion and cheese. Season with salt and pepper. Continue making layers in this way, finishing with a layer of cheese. Dot the top with margarine.

3 Beat the egg and milk together in a bowl and pour over the potatoes.

4 Cover the dish with foil and bake in the oven for 1½ hours, or until the potatoes are tender all the way through. Serve at once.

Oven-baked new potatoes

SERVES 4

750 g/1½ lb small new potatoes, scrubbed

4 sprigs of mint

4 sprigs of parsley

salt and freshly ground black pepper

25 g/1 oz butter

1 tablespoon chopped fresh mint or 1 teaspoon dried mint

1 tablespoon chopped fresh parsley

1 Heat the oven to 180C/350F/Gas 4. Put the potatoes in a 1.5 L/2½ pint casserole.

2 Tuck the mint and parsley sprigs amongst the potatoes and season with salt and pepper. Dot the butter over the top.

3 Cover the casserole and bake in the oven for 45-60 minutes until tender when pierced with a fine skewer. Using 2 spoons, turn the potatoes until evenly coated with the melted butter. Sprinkle with the chopped mint and parsley and serve at once.

Rösti

SERVES 4

500 g/1 lb potatoes, parboiled whole, cooled and skinned

1 large onion

salt and freshly ground black pepper

50 g/2 oz butter

1 Grate the potatoes and onion, season generously with salt and freshly ground black pepper and mix well.

2 Melt half the butter in a shallow frying-pan and add the potato mixture. Flatten it down with a wooden spoon or spatula and cook over moderate heat for about 5 minutes until lightly browned.

3 Put a plate on top of the pan and turn the pan over so that the potato mixture falls on to the plate. Melt the remaining butter.

4 Slide the potato back into the pan so that the underside cooks. Cook for a further 5 minutes or so. Slide on to a warmed serving plate. Serve at once.

Baked potatoes with apple

SERVES 4

4 large potatoes, each weighing about 250 g/
9 oz

½ medium cooking apple

25 g/1 oz margarine or butter

1 large onion, finely chopped

4 sage leaves, chopped, or 1 teaspoon dried
sage

½ teaspoon mustard powder

salt

margarine, for greasing

1 Heat the oven to 200C/400F/Gas 6.
2 Scrub the potatoes and with a fork prick each one in 2 places on both sides. Bake the potatoes for 1½ hours.
3 Remove the potatoes from the oven (leaving the oven on), allow to cool slightly, then cut each one in half lengthways. Scoop the cooked potato into a bowl, leaving the shells intact. Mash the potato well. Peel, core and finely chop the apple.
4 Melt the margarine in a small

Above left: The potato cake, Rösti
Above: Creamy piquant cabbage

frying-pan, add the onion and fry gently until it begins to soften, stirring occasionally. Stir in the apple and cook for 2-3 minutes, until soft.
5 Stir the apple and onion mixture into the mashed potato. Add the sage, mustard and a little salt. Mix well.
6 Spoon the mixture back into the potato shells and make criss-cross patterns on the top with a fork.
7 Put the potato shells in a greased shallow ovenproof dish and return to the oven. Bake for 15 minutes until the tops are browned. Serve at once.

Creamy piquant cabbage

SERVES 4

1 Savoy cabbage, weighing about 850 g/
1¾ lb, quartered

salt

Sauce

50 g/2 oz butter

50 g/2 oz plain flour

425 ml/¾ pint vegetable stock

150 ml/¼ pint single cream

3 tablespoons medium-dry sherry

2 teaspoons French mustard

2 tablespoons chopped fresh parsley

2 teaspoons lemon juice

freshly ground black pepper

1 Bring a pan of salted water to the boil, add the cabbage and bring back to the boil. Simmer for about 10 minutes, until the cabbage is just tender.
2 Meanwhile, make the sauce: melt the butter in a saucepan, sprinkle in the flour and stir over low heat for 1-2 minutes until straw-coloured. Gradually stir in the stock, then simmer, stirring until thick and smooth.
3 Gradually stir in the cream, sherry, mustard and parsley and heat through gently. Remove from the heat and stir in the lemon juice and salt and pepper.
4 Drain the cabbage. Transfer to a warmed serving dish, pour over the sauce and serve at once.

Chinese-style leeks

SERVES 4-6

250 g/9 oz leeks, cut into 5 cm/2 inch lengths

25 g/1 oz margarine or butter

1 onion, sliced

50 g/2 oz walnut pieces

4 celery stalks, chopped

250 g/9 oz Chinese leaves, sliced

salt and freshly ground black pepper

few dashes of soy sauce

1 Melt the margarine in a frying-pan, add the leeks and onion and fry gently for 5 minutes until the onion is soft.

2 Add the walnuts, together with the celery, and fry over moderate heat, stirring, for 3 minutes.

3 Stir the Chinese leaves into the pan and cook for a further 2 minutes, stirring constantly.

4 Season to taste with salt and pepper, stir in the soy sauce and cook for a further minute. Serve at once.

Baked red cabbage

SERVES 4

1 red cabbage, shredded

8 prunes

150 ml/¼ pint dry red wine

25 g/1 oz margarine or butter

1 large onion, thinly sliced

1 large cooking apple

1 Soak the prunes in the wine for 3 hours. Drain, reserving the wine. Halve and stone prunes.

2 Heat the oven to 180C/350F/Gas 4.

3 Melt the margarine in a flameproof casserole. Add the onion and fry gently until soft.

4 Meanwhile, peel, core and slice the apple, then add to the pan. Cook gently for about 5 minutes.

5 Stir in the cabbage and prunes. Pour in the reserved wine and bring to the boil. Cover the casserole tightly, transfer to the oven and bake for 1 hour. Serve hot.

Below: A touch of the Orient with Chinese-style leeks
Far right: Lemon gives Zesty carrots a deliciously tangy flavour

Zesty carrots

SERVES 4

750 g/1½ lb small carrots, sliced thickly
finely grated zest and juice of 1 lemon
25 g/1 oz butter
1 teaspoon light soft brown sugar
salt and freshly ground black pepper
5 tablespoons water
lemon slices and finely snipped chives, to
*   garnish*

1 Put carrot slices into a saucepan with the lemon zest and the juice, the butter, sugar, salt and pepper to taste, and the water.
2 Place the pan over high heat and bring to the boil, then cover with a tight-fitting lid. Lower the heat and simmer gently for 40 minutes, until carrots are just tender and the liquid has reduced to a glaze.
3 Turn the glazed carrots into a warmed serving dish. Garnish with lemon slices and snipped chives.

Sweet and sour carrots

SERVES 4-6

500 g/1 lb carrots, thickly sliced
salt
2 tablespoons vegetable oil
1 onion, sliced
3 celery stalks, sliced
25 g/1 oz blanched almonds, halved
Sauce
2 teaspoons soy sauce
2 teaspoons cornflour
1 tablespoon brown sugar
1 tablespoon cider vinegar
2 teaspoons lemon juice

1 Cook the carrots in boiling salted water for about 10-20 minutes until barely tender – the carrots should still be firm. Drain, reserving the stock.
2 Heat the oil in a frying-pan, add the onion and celery and fry over moderate heat for about 5 minutes, stirring constantly. Do not allow the onion and celery to turn brown.
3 Add the drained carrots to the pan and stir to coat them in oil. Remove the pan from the heat.
4 Make the sauce: mix together in a saucepan the soy sauce and cornflour, then add the sugar, vinegar and lemon juice and stir in 150 ml/¼ pint of the reserved carrot stock. Mix well.
5 Pour the sauce over the vegetables in the pan and bring to the boil, stirring all the time. Boil briskly for 3 minutes, stirring occasionally.
6 Turn the vegetables into a warmed serving dish and scatter with the almonds. Serve at once.

Stir-fried mushrooms with mange-tout

SERVES 4

250 g/9 oz button mushrooms, sliced
250 g/9 oz mange-tout peas
salt
1 small red pepper, deseeded
1 tablespoon soy sauce
1 tablespoon dry sherry
1 teaspoon clear honey
4 tablespoons sunflower oil
1 clove garlic, chopped
50 g/2 oz cashews
4 tablespoons water

1 Top and tail the mange-tout peas, string if necessary and cut into 2.5 cm/1 inch pieces. Blanch in a large pan of boiling, lightly salted water for 1½ minutes; drain, refresh in cold water and drain thoroughly again.
2 Cut the pepper into matchstick strips. In a small bowl combine the soy sauce, sherry and honey.
3 Heat the oil and garlic in a Chinese wok or large frying-pan over a moderate heat. When the garlic begins to sizzle, add the sliced mushrooms and strips of pepper and stir-fry for 2 minutes. Add the cashews and stir-fry for a further minute.
4 Add a good pinch of salt and the water and boil over high heat until the liquid has almost entirely evaporated. Stir the soy sauce mixture and pour into pan. Toss vegetables and nuts in the sauce, then add the mange-tout. Stir-fry for 1 minute. Serve.

Peas and pears in tarragon

SERVES 4

350 g/12 oz frozen peas
350 g/12 oz ripe, but firm pears
salt
25 g/1 oz butter
1-2 teaspoons dried tarragon
freshly ground black pepper
sprigs of tarragon, to garnish

Above: Stir-fried mushrooms
Far right: Peas and pears in tarragon

1 Bring a small quantity of salted water to the boil and cook the peas according to packet instructions.
2 Meanwhile, peel and core the pears and cut them into chunks. Melt the butter over very gentle heat, add the pears and fry gently for about 5 minutes until soft but not mushy. Stir in the tarragon.
3 Drain the peas and add them to the pan, season to taste with pepper, then gently mix together.
4 Turn the peas and pears into a warmed serving dish, scraping the pan to ensure the juices are added. Garnish with sprigs of tarragon and serve the dish at once.

● Tarragon has quite an unusual and distinctive aniseed flavour. If you are not familiar with the taste and are not sure how much to add, use just 1 teaspoon of dried tarragon the very first time you try making this dish.

Fried onion rings

SERVES 4

500 g/1 lb Spanish onions
50 g/2 oz wholemeal flour
¼ teaspoon bicarbonate of soda
large pinch of cream of tartar
large pinch of salt
1 egg
3 tablespoons milk
1 teaspoon melted butter
vegetable oil, for deep-frying

1 Make the batter: sift together the flour, bicarbonate of soda, cream of tartar and salt. Beat the egg and milk together, then stir in the melted butter. Add the flour mixture to the egg mixture and beat well until the batter is smooth and glossy. Set the batter aside while you prepare the onions.
2 Slice the onions into thin even rounds, then separate the rounds so that they fall into rings.
3 Heat the oven to 110C/225F/Gas ¼.
4 Heat the oil in a deep-fat frier to 190C/375F or until a cube of stale bread turns golden brown in 50 seconds: it is important to have the oil just hot enough for frying, but not so hot that it burns the onions.
5 Scoop up several onion rings on the prongs of a large fork, dip them into the batter and allow the excess batter to drain back into the bowl. Drop the coated onions rings into the hot oil and fry for 3-4 minutes, until the batter is golden brown and puffed up on each ring.
6 Remove with a slotted spoon and drain on crumpled absorbent paper. Put them on a warmed dish, cover with foil and keep hot while you fry the remainder in the same way. (If the onions should become slightly soggy while being kept warm drop them once more in the hot oil, just for a few seconds, then drain again and serve at once.)

• A handy alternative way of slicing onions into rounds is to slice them before peeling. The skin easily slips off each round.

Creamed onions

SERVES 4-6

750 g/1½ lb onions
salt
150 ml/¼ pint soured cream
freshly ground black pepper
sweet paprika
25 g/1 oz margarine or butter
4 tablespoons day-old white breadcrumbs
1 tablespoon chopped fresh parsley
2 hard-boiled eggs
parsley sprigs, to garnish

1 Cook the onions in boiling salted water for 15-20 minutes. Drain them thoroughly, reserving 1 tablespoon of the cooking liquid. Leave the onions to cool slightly, then pat them dry with absorbent paper.
2 Heat the oven to 180C/350F/Gas 4.
3 Put the onions on a board and slice them. Arrange the sliced onions in an ovenproof dish.
4 Beat the soured cream with the reserved onion liquid and season with salt, pepper and sweet paprika to taste. Pour the cream over the onions.
5 Melt the margarine in a small frying-pan, add the breadcrumbs and fry for about 5 minutes over moderate heat, stirring frequently, until they are golden and crisp.
6 Remove the pan from the heat and stir in the parsley. Chop 1 hard-boiled egg and stir it into the fried crumb mixture. Spoon the mixture evenly over the onions.
7 Bake in the oven for 15 minutes. Meanwhile, slice the remaining hard-boiled egg.
8 Arrange the egg slices in a row along the top of the dish. Sprinkle with paprika, garnish with parsley and serve at once.

Mushrooms in vine leaves

SERVES 4

8 large flat mushrooms

12-18 vine leaves in brine, drained

4 tablespoons olive oil

2 teaspoons finely chopped fresh marjoram

salt and freshly ground black pepper

1   Heat the oven to 180C/350F/Gas 4.

2   Rinse the vine leaves under cold running water, pat dry with absorbent paper, then lay half the vine leaves over the bottom of an ovenproof dish or roasting tin. Sprinkle 1 tablespoon of the oil over the vine leaves.

3   Leaving the mushrooms whole, lay them on top of the vine leaves, stalk-side up. Sprinkle with the remaining oil and the marjoram, then season to taste with salt and pepper. Cover with the rest of the vine leaves.

4   Bake for 30-40 minutes.

5   Remove and discard the top layer of vine leaves, then divide the mushrooms and remaining leaves between 4 individual plates. Serve.

Turnip and potato clapshot

SERVES 4

350 g/12 oz small turnips, cut into chunks

500 g/1 lb potatoes, cut into chunks

salt

25 g/1 oz butter

freshly ground black pepper

2 tablespoons snipped chives

1   Bring the turnips to the boil in a large saucepan of salted water. Lower the heat and simmer for 5 minutes. Add the potatoes, return to the boil, then simmer for a further 10-15 minutes until the vegetables are tender.

2   Drain the vegetables well and mash to a fine purée. Beat in the butter, then season to taste with salt and pepper. Alternatively, put the drained potatoes and turnips with the butter and seasoning into the goblet of a blender and work until the mixture is completely smooth.

3   Turn the apuréed vegetables into a warmed serving dish and sprinkle with snipped chives. Serve at once.

Tomato braised celery

SERVES 4

2 large heads celery

salt

25 g/1 oz margarine or butter

1 onion, chopped

500 g/1 lb tomatoes, skinned and sliced

freshly ground black pepper

2 tablespoons finely chopped fresh parsley

2 tablespoons sliced stuffed olives, to garnish (optional)

grated Parmesan cheese, to serve

1   Cut off the root end off the celery and discard it. Cut off the leaves and pull away the stringy, outer stalks. Wash the celery under cold, running water – brush the stalks with a small hard brush while washing them.

2   Cut the celery into 7.5 cm/3 inch pieces. Bring a pan of salted water to the boil add the celery and simmer gently for 3 minutes. Drain the celery thoroughly.

3   Melt the margarine in a saucepan, add the onion and fry gently for 3-4

minutes, until soft but not coloured. Add the tomatoes, stir well and simmer for 3 minutes. Add the celery, season with salt and freshly ground black pepper to taste and stir in the chopped parsley. Cover the pan and continue to simmer for a further 10 minutes, or until the celery is tender. Test by piercing with a sharp knife.

4 Turn the vegetables into a warmed serving dish, garnish with the olives, if using, and serve at once with cheese.

Peppers in tomato juice

SERVES 4

250 g/9 oz green peppers, deseeded and sliced
250 g/9 oz red peppers, deseeded and sliced
1 tablespoon vegetable oil
25 g/1 oz butter
1 small onion, finely chopped
1 clove garlic, crushed (optional)
1 teaspoon dried rosemary
½ teaspoon sugar
300 ml/½ pint tomato juice
salt and freshly ground black pepper

1 Heat the oil and butter in a frying-pan, add the onion and fry gently for 5 minutes until soft and lightly coloured. Add the peppers and garlic, if using, and fry for a further 5 minutes, stirring occasionally.
2 Stir half the rosemary and the sugar into the tomato juice. Season with salt and pepper; pour into pan.
3 Simmer, uncovered, for about 10 minutes, stirring occasionally, until the peppers are tender and the tomato juice has reduced to a sauce. Transfer to warmed dish, sprinkle with remaining rosemary and serve at once.

Baked parsnips with soured cream

SERVES 4

500 g/1 lb parsnips, sliced
2 tablespoons vegetable oil
1 large onion, sliced
300 ml/½ pint vegetable stock
½ teaspoon English made mustard
¼ teaspoon sweet paprika
150 ml/¼ pint soured cream

Above left: Mushrooms in vine leaves
Above: Peppers in tomato juice

Topping
50 g/2 oz wholemeal breadcrumbs
25 g/1 oz Cheddar cheese, grated

1 Heat the oven to 200C/400F/Gas 6.
2 Heat the oil in a large frying-pan, add the onion and fry gently for 5 minutes until soft and lightly coloured. Add the parsnips and continue frying gently for 3-4 minutes until the parsnips are beginning to soften.
3 Stir in the stock, mustard and paprika. Bring to the boil, then lower the heat slightly and simmer for 15 minutes. Remove from the heat and stir in the soured cream with a wooden spoon until it is thoroughly combined. Spoon the mixture into an ovenproof dish. Set aside.
4 Make the topping: mix the brown breadcrumbs with the cheese and sprinkle over the top of the parsnip and soured cream mixture.
5 Bake in the oven for 1 hour until crisp and golden on top. Serve at once, straight from the dish.

Curried spinach

SERVES 4

1 kg/2 lb fresh spinach, stalks and coarse
    midribs removed, or 500 g/1 lb block frozen
    leaf spinach, defrosted and drained
2 tablespoons vegetable oil
1 onion, chopped
1 large clove garlic, crushed
1 teaspoon ground coriander
1 teaspoon ground cumin
1/2 teaspoon ground turmeric
1/4 teaspoon ground ginger
1/4 teaspoon chilli powder
1/2 teaspoon salt
1 tablespoon lemon juice

1 Heat the oil in a large frying-pan,
add the onion and garlic and fry gently
for 5 minutes until soft.
2 Add spices and salt and fry for 5
minutes, stirring constantly.

3 Shake the spinach well and add to
the pan with only the water that still
clings to the leaves. Add the lemon
juice and cook for 10 minutes over
moderate heat, turning the spinach
until it softens.
4 Transfer to a warmed serving dish
and serve at once.

Okra Mediterranean-style

SERVES 4

500 g/1 lb okra, ends trimmed and blemishes
    removed
4 tablespoons vegetable oil
1 large onion, chopped
500 g/1 lb tomatoes, skinned and quartered
1 clove garlic, crushed
1 teaspoon ground coriander
salt and freshly ground black pepper
coriander leaves, to garnish

1 Heat the oil in a large saucepan,
add onion and fry for 5 minutes.
2 Add the okra to the pan, stir to coat
well with the oil, then add the tomatoes, garlic and coriander. Stir well to
mix, then season to taste.
3 Bring to the boil, then lower the
heat slightly, cover and simmer for 30
minutes until okra is tender. Serve
garnished with coriander.

Nutty courgettes

SERVES 4

750 g/1 1/2 lb courgettes, cut into 5 mm/1/4 inch
    slices
25 g/1 oz margarine or butter
2 cloves garlic, crushed
75 g/3 oz shelled walnuts, roughly chopped
generous pinch of salt
freshly ground black pepper

1 Melt the margarine in a frying-pan, add the crushed garlic and fry gently for 1-2 minutes, until soft and lightly coloured.

2 Add the sliced courgettes, stir well to coat thoroughly in the margarine, then fry over low heat for 10 minutes, turning occasionally.

3 Add the chopped walnuts, the salt and a generous sprinkling of black pepper. Cook for a further 5 minutes until the courgettes are tender, stirring occasionally. Transfer to a warmed serving dish and serve at once.

Spicy red beans

SERVES 4

250 g/9 oz red kidney beans, soaked overnight
2 tablespoons vegetable oil
2 onions, thinly sliced
1 clove garlic, chopped (optional)
1/2 teaspoon ground mixed spice
1/4 teaspoon cayenne pepper
600 ml/1 pint vegetable stock
2 tablespoons tomato purée
2 tablespoons white wine vinegar
1 bay leaf
salt

1 Drain the soaked beans, rinse under cold running water, then place in a large saucepan and cover with fresh cold water. Bring to the boil, boil for 15 minutes, then drain the beans thoroughly.

2 Heat the oven to 180C/350F/Gas 4.

3 Heat the oil in a flameproof casserole, add the sliced onions, chopped garlic, if using, mixed spice and cayenne pepper and fry over low heat for about 10 minutes until the onions are soft but not coloured.

4 Stir the beans into the casserole. Pour in the stock, increase the heat and bring to the boil. Add the tomato purée, vinegar, bay leaf and a pinch of salt. Stir to mix well.

5 Cover the casserole and transfer to the oven. Cook for about 2 hours until the beans are soft and most of the stock is absorbed.

6 Discard the bay leaf, then taste and adjust seasoning. Serve the beans hot, straight from the casserole.

Left: Curried spinach
Right: Nutty courgettes

Desserts

To complete a vegetarian meal, why not treat family and friends to a special dessert? Our selection includes glamorous creamy creations, as well as cool ices and fruity puddings.

Rich chocolate mousse

SERVES 6-8

50 g/2 oz plain dark chocolate, broken into small pieces

3 tablespoons hot water

75 g/3 oz caster sugar

5 eggs, separated

100 g/4 oz unsalted cashew nuts, finely ground

300 ml/½ pint double cream

pinch of salt

few whole cashew nuts, to decorate

1 Put the chocolate in the top of a double boiler or a bowl set over a saucepan of simmering water. Add the water and sugar and stir with a wooden spoon over low heat until the chocolate is completely melted and the sugar fully dissolved.

2 Remove from the heat. Remove the top section of the double boiler or the bowl from the hot water. Using a balloon whisk, beat in the egg yolks one at a time, beating well after each addition. Set the chocolate mixture aside to cool for about 15 minutes.

3 Lightly stir the ground cashew nuts into cooled chocolate mixture.

4 Put 225 ml/8 fl oz of the cream and the egg whites in separate clean dry bowls. Whip the cream until standing in soft peaks. Whisk the egg whites until standing in stiff peaks. Lightly fold first the cream, then the whisked egg whites into the chocolate mixture.

5 Pour the mixture into a glass serving bowl, cover with cling film and refrigerate overnight or until set.

6 Just before serving, whip the remaining cream until standing in soft peaks. Pipe rosettes of cream around the edge of the mousse and top each rosette with a cashew nut. Serve.

Gooseberry fool

SERVES 6

500 g/1 lb green gooseberries

50 g/2 oz Barbados sugar

½ teaspoon ground cinnamon

pinch of ground cloves

4 tablespoons water

300 ml/½ pint double cream

mint leaves, to decorate

1 Top and tail the gooseberries. Put them in a large saucepan with the sugar, spices and water. Cover and cook over a low heat for 20 minutes or until the fruit is very soft.

2 Put the cooked gooseberries into a bowl and break them up with a fork, but do not reduce them to a purée.

3 Whip the cream until standing in soft peaks, then gently fold into the gooseberries with a metal spoon.

4 Pile the fool into one large glass bowl or 6 individual bowls. Refrigerate for 1 hour, and decorate with mint leaves before serving.

Honeyed apricot whips

SERVES 4

100 g/4 oz dried apricots

300 ml/½ pint hot water

2 tablespoons clear honey

300 g/10 oz natural yoghurt

2 egg whites

boudoir biscuits or chocolate fingers, to serve

1 Put the apricots in a small bowl with the hot water and leave to soak for at least 4 hours or, if possible, overnight.

2 Turn the apricots and water into a heavy-based saucepan. Add the honey, cover and simmer very gently for about 20 minutes, until the apricots are tender. Remove from the heat and leave to cool completely.

3 Purée the apricots with the cooking syrup and yoghurt in a blender.

4 Whisk the egg whites until they stand in soft peaks. Using a metal spoon, lightly stir 1 tablespoon of the whisked egg whites into the apricot purée mixture, then fold in the remainder.

5 Spoon the whip into stemmed glasses. Serve at once, or refrigerate until serving time. Serve with the biscuits.

Sparkling syllabub

SERVES 2

1 thin strip lemon rind

2 tablespoons lemon juice

2 tablespoons brandy

2 tablespoons caster sugar

4 tablespoons sparkling dry white wine, chilled

175 ml/6 fl oz double cream

1 Put the lemon rind, lemon juice, brandy and caster sugar into a bowl. Cover and leave to stand for at least 3 hours.

2 Remove the lemon rind, pour in the wine and stir in the double cream.

3 Using a hand whisk, beat the mixture until it is light and fluffy and will hold soft peaks. Divide the mixture equally between 2 large glasses, then refrigerate for 30-60 minutes. Serve chilled.

Glamorous Rich chocolate mousse

Coeurs à la crème

SERVES 2

100 g/4 oz curd cheese

1 tablespoon caster sugar

finely grated zest of ½ lemon

150 ml/¼ pint double cream

1 egg white

250 g/9 oz fresh or frozen small strawberries or raspberries

extra caster sugar, for sweetening

1 Line 2 heart-shaped *coeurs à la crème* moulds with large squares of wet muslin: wet muslin helps prevent the cheese mixture from sticking. Allow the muslin to hang over sides.

2 Pass the curd cheese through a nylon sieve into a bowl, add the caster sugar and lemon zest and beat well until very soft.

3 Whisk 4 tablespoons of the cream until it forms soft peaks, then mix into the cheese mixture.

4 Whisk the egg white in a clean, dry bowl until it stands in stiff peaks. Fold 1 tablespoon of the egg white into the cheese mixture to lighten it, then fold in the rest.

5 Spoon the cheese mixture into the prepared moulds and smooth the tops. Fold the overhanging pieces of muslin over the cheese mixture to enclose it completely. Put the moulds on a flat plate and refrigerate them overnight.

6 About 1 hour before serving, sprinkle the strawberries with caster sugar to sweeten.

7 To serve: remove the moulds from the refrigerator and unwrap the tops. Place a small serving plate on top of each mould, then carefully invert the plate and mould together. Shake gently, unmould, then carefully remove the muslin.

8 Decorate with some of the fruit, then pour over the remaining unwhipped cream. Put the remaining fruit in empty moulds and serve separately.

● Coeurs à la crème moulds are available from kitchen equipment stores. The moulds are heart-shaped with raised, perforated bases.

Rum and raisin cheesecake

SERVES 6

175 g/6 oz plain chocolate-coated wheatmeal biscuits, finely crushed

75 g/3 oz butter, melted

butter, for greasing

Filling

350 g/12 oz full-fat soft cheese

2 tablespoons caster sugar

2 eggs, beaten

1-2 tablespoons dark rum

3 tablespoons seedless raisins

Topping

1 teaspoon caster sugar

150 ml/¼ pint soured cream

50 g/2 oz seedless raisins

50 ml/2 fl oz dark rum

1 Grease a 19 cm/7½ inch round loose-bottomed cake tin.

2 Mix the crushed biscuits with the melted butter until evenly combined, then spoon into the greased tin and press evenly and firmly over the base. Refrigerate for 30 minutes.

3 Heat the oven to 170C/325F/Gas 3. Make the filling: Beat the soft cheese with a wooden spoon until creamy and smooth, then slowly beat in the caster sugar and eggs. Add rum to taste, then stir in the raisins.

4 Pour the cheese mixture into the prepared tin and bake in the oven for about 40 minutes, until set. Turn off the oven heat and leave the cheesecake to cool in the oven, with the door ajar, for 1 hour.

5 Make the topping: stir the caster sugar into the soured cream, then spread the cream over the top of the cooled cheesecake, taking it almost to the edges. Cover and refrigerate for at least 2 hours. Meanwhile, combine the raisins and rum and leave to soak until required.

6 To serve: remove the sides of the tin by placing the tin on an inverted pudding basin and easing the sides down. Place the cheesecake on a serving plate and sprinkle the soaked raisins around the edge of the soured cream. Serve.

Pashka

SERVES 16

1.5 kg/3 lb 5 oz cottage or curd cheese
100 g/4 oz blanched almonds, chopped
100 g/4 oz candied mixed peel, chopped
200 g/7 oz seedless raisins, chopped
100 g/4 oz glacé cherries, chopped
250 g/9 oz butter, softened
3 eggs
200 g/7 oz caster sugar
100 ml/4 fl oz clotted, double or soured
  cream
1 teaspoon rose-water

To decorate

blanched almonds
glacé cherries
candied fruit
angelica

1 Put the cottage or curd cheese in a cheesecloth bag and hang over the sink for at least 12 hours to drain.

2 Rub the drained cheese through a sieve into a bowl. Mix the chopped almonds and candied peel, raisins and cherries with the softened butter, and mix into the cheese.

3 Whisk the eggs with the sugar until they are pale yellow and frothy, then mix them into the cottage cheese mixture, whisking thoroughly to eliminate lumps. Whisk in the cream and rose-water and continue to mix until completely smooth.

4 Line a flowerpot large enough to hold the pudding with scalded cheesecloth, leaving plenty of material round the edge to fold over the top.

5 Pour the pashka mixture into the lined flowerpot, then fold the edges of the cloth neatly over the top of the pot.

Far left: Creamy Coeurs à la crème, perfect for that romantic occasion
Above: Rich and irresistible, Rum and raisin cheesecake

Place a small plate inside the pot and weight down.

6 Put the flowerpot on a wire rack in a shallow dish so as much liquid as possible drains from the pashka. Refrigerate for at least 12 hours.

7 Remove the weight and plate. To unmould: invert a round serving plate on top of the flowerpot, then gently invert, holding pot and plate firmly. Carefully remove the flowerpot and peel away the cheesecloth.

8 Decorate the top and sides of the pashka with almonds, cherries, candied fruit and angelica. Press gently but firmly into surface, so they adhere.

Pineapple cheesecake

SERVES 10

75 g/3 oz butter, melted

175 g/6 oz wheatmeal biscuits, crushed

1 tablespoon grated lemon zest

300 g/11 oz caster sugar

250 g/9 oz can crushed pineapple in syrup, well drained

750 g/1½ lb curd cheese, sieved

1 teaspoon salt

25 g/1 oz plain flour

3 tablespoons lemon juice

100 ml/4 fl oz double cream

4 eggs

extra crushed pineapple, to decorate

To decorate

150 ml/¼ pint double cream

canned pineapple chunks, halved

1   Heat the oven to 170C/325F/Gas 3.

2   Make the crust: stir the melted butter into the biscuit crumbs, then thoroughly mix in 1 teaspoon grated lemon zest and 50 g/2 oz sugar. Reserve 4 tablespoons of the mixture and use the rest to line a 23 cm/9 inch spring-release tin. Cover the crust with the crushed pineapple.

3   Put the curd cheese in a bowl and add the salt, flour, remaining lemon zest, lemon juice and cream. Beat well.

4   Beat the eggs with the remaining sugar until the mixture is light and fluffy, then fold into the cheese mixture.

5   Pour the filling into the tin and sprinkle the top with the reserved crumb mixture.

6   Bake in the oven for 1 hour, then turn off the heat and let the cake stand in the oven for 1 hour. Transfer to a wire rack and allow to cool completely before removing the rim of the tin.

7   To decorate: whip the cream until standing in soft peaks, then pipe a cream shell border around the edge of the cheesecake. Spike the cream with pineapple chunk halves and serve at once.

Yorkshire curd tarts

MAKES 10

shortcrust pastry, made with 100 g/4 oz wholemeal flour (page 42)

Filling

25 g/1 oz margarine

25 g/1 oz caster sugar

100 g/4 oz cottage cheese, sieved

1 egg, beaten

grated zest and juice of ½ lemon

4 teaspoons top of the milk

50 g/2 oz currants

1   Heat the oven to 200C/400F/Gas 6.

2   On a lightly floured surface, roll out the pastry, then cut into as many rounds as possible using a 7.5 cm/3 inch pastry cutter. Knead the trimmings together, roll out and cut again to make 10 rounds altogether.

3   Line ten 6 cm/2½ inch tart moulds with the pastry rounds. Refrigerate while you make the filling.

4   Beat the margarine with the sugar until pale and fluffy, then stir in the cheese. Add the egg, lemon zest and juice, top of the milk and currants and mix well.

5   Divide the filling equally between the pastry-lined moulds. Bake in the oven for 20-25 minutes, until the filling is puffing up.

6   Cool the tarts for 2-3 minutes, then remove from the moulds with the aid of a small palette knife. Leave on a wire rack to cool.

Cassata siciliana

SERVES 8

400 g/14 oz Ricotta cheese

150 ml/¼ pint water

175 g/6 oz caster sugar

200 g/7 oz best-quality crystallized fruit

pinch of ground cinnamon

75 g/3 oz bitter chocolate, cut into small pieces

25 g/1 oz pistachio nuts, chopped

100 ml/4 fl oz Maraschino or another sweet liqueur such as curaçao or Drambuie

500 g/1 lb Madeira cake

Icing

600 g/1¼ lb icing sugar, sifted

100 ml/3½ fl oz water

1 tablespoon lemon juice

1 Press the Ricotta cheese through a fine-mesh sieve and set aside. Pour the water into a heavy-based saucepan and add the sugar. Heat gently until the sugar has dissolved. Bring to the boil, without stirring, and boil for 1 minute until a clear syrup is formed. Do not stir during boiling.

2 Meanwhile, cut 100 g/4 oz of the crystallized fruit into small pieces, reserving the best pieces for decoration.

3 Remove the syrup from heat, pour it over the Ricotta and stir vigorously until the mixture is glossy and smooth. Add the cinnamon, chocolate, chopped crystallized fruit, pistachios and half the liqueur and mix thoroughly with a wooden spoon.

4 Line an 18 cm/7 inch deep round cake tin with greaseproof paper. Cut the Madeira cake into thin slices and use about two-thirds to line the bottom and the sides of the tin. Use the trimmings to fill in any gaps. Sprinkle over some of the liqueur to moisten the cake.

5 Spoon in the Ricotta mixture and cover it with a layer of sliced cake. Moisten the top layer with the remaining liqueur. Cover with cling film and refrigerate for at least 3 hours.

6 Make the icing: melt the icing sugar with the water and the lemon juice in a heavy-based saucepan over low heat until it evenly coats the back of a spoon.

7 Turn the cake out on to a flat plate or cake board, pour the icing over the cake and let it run down the sides. Smooth the icing with a slightly warmed palette knife.

8 Return the cake to the refrigerator for at least 5 minutes to allow the icing to set. Transfer the cake to a serving plate and decorate with the reserved crystallized fruit in the centre. Serve the cassata at once.

Fresh orange jelly

SERVES 4

5 large oranges

100 g/4 oz cube sugar

225 ml/8 fl oz water

2 teaspoons agar-agar

1 tablespoon Cointreau or Grand Marnier liqueur (optional)

fresh orange slices, to decorate

1 Chill a 600 ml/1 pint metal mould in the refrigerator. Wash and dry the oranges. Rub the sugar cubes over the orange skins to extract the essence from the zest and place the sugar in a heavy-based saucepan. Add half the water and stir over a low heat until the sugar is completely dissolved. Remove the sugar syrup from the heat and set aside until needed.

2 Squeeze the juice from the oranges, strain and measure out 350 ml/12 fl oz, making up this quantity with a little water if necessary. Combine the orange juice with the sugar syrup, then pour into a jelly bag or muslin-lined sieve suspended over a clean bowl. Leave for about 30 minutes to drip through.

3 Sprinkle the agar-agar over the remaining water in a small pan and stir to mix well. Boil gently, until dissolved. Allow to cool slightly, then pour in a thin stream on to the strained orange juice, stirring constantly. Stir

Far left: Cassata siciliana makes a glamorous dinner party dessert
Above: Fresh orange jelly tastes refreshing and looks stunning

in the liqueur if using.

4 Rinse out the chilled mould with cold water and pour in the strained orange mixture. Cover and refrigerate for about 8 hours or overnight, until the orange jelly is set firm.

5 To unmould: wring a cloth out in hot water and hold it around the mould for a few seconds, then invert a chilled, lightly moistened serving plate on top of the mould. Hold the plate and mould firmly and quickly invert them, giving a sharp jerk half-way over. When the mould and plate are completely inverted, give them a firm shake. Carefully unmould.

6 Arrange the orange slices around the base of the jelly in an overlapping pattern, just before serving.

cream until just thickened. Stir the frothy meringue mixture, then whisk into the cream, about one-third at a time. Pour the syllabub over the biscuits and grapes, cover the glasses with cling film and refrigerate for 1-2 hours, until the biscuits are moistened and softened. Do not chill for too long or liquid will collect in the bottom of the glass.

4 Just before serving, top each syllabub with slices of kiwi fruit. (If added too far in advance, the slices will lose their freshness.) Serve chilled.

Dried fruit salad

SERVES 6-8

500 g/1 lb dried apricots (sharp rather than sweet)
250 g/9 oz prunes
100 g/4 oz raisins or sultanas
100 g/4 oz blanched almonds, halved
50 g/2 oz pistachios, halved, or pine nuts
175 g/6 oz sugar
2 tablespoons rose-water or orange blossom water

1 Put the dried apricots in a large bowl, together with the prunes, raisins, almonds, pistachios, sugar and rose-water.

2 Pour in enough water to cover and leave for at least 48 hours, to allow the fruit to plump up and the flavours to blend.

3 Serve the salad with some of its syrup poured over the top.

Spiced pears

SERVES 6

6 firm pears
425 ml/3/4 pint dry cider
75 g/3 oz apricot jam, sieved
40 g/11/2 oz soft brown sugar
1/4 teaspoon ground cinnamon
2 whole cloves
thin strips of orange zest
juice of 1/2 lemon

1 Put the cider in a deep saucepan, together with the jam, sugar, cinnamon and cloves. Bring the mixture slowly to the boil.

Grape syllabub

SERVES 6-8

500 g/1 lb grapes, halved with seeds removed
100 g/4 oz macaroons, coarsely crushed
2 large egg whites
100 g/4 oz caster sugar
125 ml/4 fl oz medium dry white wine
2 tablespoons brandy or sherry
300 ml/1/2 pint double cream
2 kiwi fruits, peeled and sliced, to decorate

1 Divide half the grapes equally between 6-8 tall stemmed dessert glasses, then cover with half the crushed macaroons. Place the rest of the grapes on top and finish with a layer of the remaining macaroons.

2 In a clean, dry, large bowl, whisk the egg whites until standing in stiff peaks. Add half the sugar and whisk until the meringue is stiff and glossy. Using a large metal spoon, fold in the remaining sugar. Gradually fold and stir in the wine and brandy.

3 In a separate large bowl, whip the

2 Peel the pears, leaving them whole and with the stalks on. Immediately stand them upright in the saucepan, add the orange zest and lemon juice, cover tightly and simmer gently for 20-30 minutes or until just tender but not too soft.

3 Cut a thin slice from the base of each pear. Stand the pears upright in a serving dish. Boil the liquid in the uncovered saucepan for about 10 minutes to reduce by half. Strain and pour over the pears. Leave overnight in the refrigerator. About 1 hour before serving, baste the pears well with the syrup.

Peaches Gorgonzola

SERVES 4

5 fresh peaches, skinned
3 tablespoons brandy
25 g/1 oz mashed Gorgonzola or Dolcelatte, rind removed
2 tablespoons double cream
1 tablespoon icing sugar

1 Halve and stone peaches. Put 8 peach halves in a bowl; sprinkle with 1 tablespoon brandy. Leave for 1-2 hours.

2 Blend the remaining 2 peach halves with the cheese or pass through a vegetable mill. Add the remaining brandy, cream and icing sugar. Blend until smooth. Refrigerate for 1 hour.

3 Divide the peach halves between individual glasses and top with brandied cheese cream. Serve at once.

Peaches and raspberries in wine

SERVES 4-6

4-6 large peaches, or 8-10 small ones
250 g/9 oz fresh raspberries
250 g/9 oz sugar
300 ml/½ pint water
2 cloves
3 sticks cinnamon
2-3 strips thinly pared lemon zest
2-3 strips thinly pared orange zest
300 ml/½ pint white wine
whipped double cream, to serve

Far left: Grape syllabub
Above: Peaches and raspberries in wine

1 Place the sugar in a wide saucepan with the water and stir over a gentle heat until the sugar has dissolved. Add the cloves, cinnamon sticks and strips of lemon and orange zest and bring to the boil. Carefully lower the peaches into the syrup, reduce the heat and simmer, uncovered, for 5 minutes.

2 Add the wine to the pan and continue to simmer for a further 5-10 minutes, until the peaches are soft but not mushy. Remove the pan from the heat and take out the peaches with a slotted spoon.

3 Carefully peel off the skins with your fingers, then arrange the whole peaches in a shallow glass serving dish. Decorate the peaches with the raspberries.

4 Return the pan of syrup to the heat and simmer until the liquid has reduced to 300 ml/½ pint. Spoon the hot syrup over the fruit and leave to cool, then refrigerate.

5 Serve the dessert very cold, with whipped cream.

Greengage purée

SERVES 4

1 kg/2 ¼ lb greengages, halved and stoned

50 g/2 oz sugar

500 ml/16 fl oz water

1 cinnamon stick (optional)

1 Put the sugar and water in a large heavy-based saucepan. Heat gently until the sugar has dissolved, then add the cinnamon stick, if using. Bring slowly to the boil and boil rapidly for 2 minutes to make syrup.

2 Remove the pan from the heat and add the greengages, skin-side down. Return the pan to the heat and simmer the greengages for 15 minutes until they are soft and pulpy.

3 Lift out the greengages with a slotted spoon and work them through a nylon sieve. Cool, then refrigerate for at least 2 hours.

Date and walnut baked apples

SERVES 4

4 large cooking apples, each weighing about 200 g/7 oz

6 tablespoons natural, unsweetened apple juice

Filling

50 g/2 oz dates, stoned and coarsely chopped

15 g/½ oz shelled walnuts, chopped

25 g/1 oz Demerara sugar

½ teaspoon ground cinnamon

1 Heat the oven to 180C/350F/Gas 4.

2 Using an apple corer or a small sharp knife, remove the core from each apple. Score the skin around the middle of each apple with a sharp knife.

3 Make the filling: mix together the dates, walnuts, sugar and ground cinnamon in a bowl. Use to fill cavities, pressing down firmly with the back of a teaspoon.

4 Place in an ovenproof dish, then pour apple juice around apples.

5 Bake in oven for 50-60 minutes, basting occasionally with the apple juice, until the apples are soft when pierced through the centre with a sharp knife. Serve at once.

Spicy apple crunch

SERVES 4

750 g/1½ lb cooking apples
1 tablespoon light soft brown sugar
1 teaspoon ground cinnamon
2 tablespoons water
margarine, for greasing

Topping
75 g/3 oz porridge oats
50 g/2 oz light soft brown sugar
25 g/1 oz wholemeal flour
¼ teaspoon salt
40 g/1½ oz margarine, melted

1 Heat the oven to 190C/375F/Gas 5.
2 Grease a shallow 1.5 L/2½ pint ovenproof dish thoroughly with margarine. Peel, quarter and core the apples, then slice them thinly. Mix the sugar with the cinnamon. Layer the apple slices in the dish, sprinkling the spiced sugar mixture in between. Sprinkle over the water.
3 Make the topping: mix the oats, sugar, flour and salt in a bowl. Stir in the melted margarine with a knife until thoroughly mixed.
4 Sprinkle the topping evenly over the apples. Bake in the oven for 50-60 minutes, until the apples are very tender and the topping is crisp and browned.
5 Serve the pudding hot or warm, straight from the dish.

Apple layer pudding

SERVES 4

1 kg/2 lb cooking apples, sliced
100 g/4 oz caster sugar
juice and finely grated zest of 1 large orange
150 g/5 oz fresh wholemeal breadcrumbs
100 g/4 oz soft brown sugar
1 teaspoon ground cinnamon
margarine, for greasing
whipped double cream, to decorate

1 Heat the oven to 200C/400F/Gas 6. Grease a baking tray.
2 Put the apples into a saucepan with the sugar and the orange juice. Cook over gentle heat for about 10 minutes until the apples are soft, then remove from the heat and beat to a smooth purée. Leave to cool.
3 Meanwhile, mix together the breadcrumbs and brown sugar and spread over the greased baking tray. Heat through in the oven, for about 15 minutes, turning every 4-5 minutes, until the sugar has caramelized and the crumbs have turned dark brown. Leave to cool.
4 When the breadcrumbs are cold, put them in a polythene bag and crush them to small crumbs using a rolling pin. Mix the grated orange zest and cinnamon into the crumbs.
5 To assemble: divide half the apple purée into individual glass bowls, then divide half the crushed crumbs over the apple. Spoon the remaining apple on top and finish with the remaining crumbs.
6 Top each serving with cream and refrigerate until ready to serve.

Far left: Date and walnut baked apples
Above: Spicy apple crunch

Wheatmeal vinegar pie

SERVES 6-8

25 g/1 oz wheatmeal flour

1 teaspoon ground mixed spice

pinch of salt

4 egg yolks

175 g/6 oz light Barbados sugar or light soft brown sugar

200 ml/7 fl oz soured cream

3 tablespoons cider vinegar

40 g/1½ oz butter, melted

200 g/7 oz sultanas

2 egg whites

soured cream, to serve

Wheatmeal pastry

250 g/9 oz wheatmeal flour

1 teaspoon salt

150 g/5 oz margarine or butter, diced

4 tablespoons iced water

1 Make the pastry: sift the flour and salt into a bowl. Add the margarine and rub in until the mixture resembles fine breadcrumbs. Stir in enough iced water to bind the ingredients together, then wrap in cling film and refrigerate for 15 mintues.

2 Heat the oven to 230C/450F/Gas 8. Roll out the pastry and use to line a 25 cm/10 inch diameter tart tin.

3 Make the filling: sift the flour with the mixed spice and salt. Place the egg yolks and sugar in a bowl and beat with an electric beater for about 10 minutes, or until the mixture is pale and thick, and leaves a trail.

4 Stir in the flour mixture, soured cream, cider vinegar and melted butter. Beat until smooth, then add the sultanas.

5 Whisk the egg whites until standing in stiff peaks and fold them in. Pour the mixture into the pastry shell, making sure the sultanas are evenly distributed.

6 Bake in the oven for 10 minutes, then lower the heat to 180C/350F/Gas 4 and cook for a further 20 minutes, until the filling is firm and browned. Serve the pie warm, accompanied by a bowl of soured cream.

Redcurrant sorbet

SERVES 4

500 g/1 lb redcurrants

100 ml/3½ fl oz water

75 g/3 oz sugar

4 tablespoons red wine

1 tablespoon icing sugar, sieved

1 egg white

To finish

caster sugar

redcurrants or mint leaves

1 Pour the water into a heavy-based saucepan and add the sugar. Heat gently until the sugar has dissolved, then increase the heat and boil the syrup for 3 minutes. Cool and set aside.

2 Put the redcurrants in a large saucepan with the wine. Cover and cook gently over a low heat for 15 minutes or until the fruit is soft and very juicy.

3 Rub the redcurrants through a fine sieve into a bowl, making sure no seeds pass through with the juice. Stir the icing sugar into the purée, then stir in the sugar syrup.

4 Pour the mixture into a freezerproof container and freeze for about 1 hour until slushy.

5 Transfer the mixture into a large mixing bowl, and whisk until it becomes light in colour. In a clean, dry bowl, whisk the egg white until standing in stiff peaks, then fold into the whisked mixture.

6 Pour the mixture back into the freezerproof container and freeze for a further 1½ hours, until it is just firm. Whisk up again in the mixing bowl, then pour back into the container and cover with a lid or foil. Freeze for a further 30 minutes.

Hazelnut and raspberry meringue

SERVES 4

100 g/4 oz hazelnuts, skinned and crushed
500 g/1 lb fresh raspberries, hulled
4 large egg whites
250 g/9 oz caster sugar
½ teaspoon malt vinegar
1 teaspoon rose-water
425 ml/¾ pint double cream
2 tablespoons kirsch
margarine, for greasing
flour, for dusting

1 Heat the oven to 190C/375F/Gas 5.
2 Grease and flour two 22 cm/8½ inch round sandwich tins. Line the base of each tin with a circle of non-stick parchment or foil.
3 Whisk the egg whites in a clean, dry bowl until standing in stiff peaks. Gradually whisk in 225 g/8 oz of the sugar, 1 tablespoon at a time, until meringue is very stiff. Whisk in the vinegar and rose-water.
4 Carefully fold the nuts into the meringue with a metal spoon, then divide the mixture equally between the prepared tins and smooth the tops. Bake in the oven, just above and just below centre, until the meringues are lightly browned, changing them over halfway through baking.
5 Remove the meringues from the oven and immediately run a palette knife around the sides to loosen them. Leave to cool for a few minutes, then carefully turn them out on to a wire rack. Loosen the paper on the bottoms with a palette knife, then turn the meringues the right side up and leave to cool completely.
6 Whip the cream with the kirsch and remaining 25 g/1 oz caster sugar until thick, but not buttery.
7 Invert 1 meringue round on to a flat serving plate, then peel off the lining paper. Spread with about one-third of the cream, then arrange the raspberries on top, reserving a few for decoration.
8 Peel the lining paper off the remaining meringue and place on top of the raspberries, flattest side up.
9 Cover the top and sides completely with the remaining cream, swirling it attractively with a palette knife. Decorate the top with the reserved raspberries, then refrigerate for up to 2 hours until serving.

Hot lemon soufflé

SERVES 4

3-4 lemons
3 large eggs, separated
4 tablespoons icing sugar
2 tablespoons plain flour
225 ml/8 fl oz milk
1 large egg white
pinch of salt
butter, for greasing
sugar, for dusting

1 Generously grease a 1.1 L/2 pint soufflé dish with butter, paying particular attention to the rim. Coat with sugar, tipping out any excess. Heat the oven to 220C/425F/Gas 7.
2 Grate the zest from 1 lemon and squeeze the remaining lemons to give 50 ml/2 fl oz lemon juice. Reserve.
3 Put the egg yolks in a heavy-based saucepan and stir lightly with a wooden spoon to break them up. Sift in the icing sugar and beat until smooth. Sift in the flour and blend lightly until the mixture is smooth and free of lumps.

Far left: Wheatmeal vinegar pie makes a wholesome family dessert
Above. When you want to impress, serve Hot lemon soufflé

4 Put the milk in another pan and heat almost to boiling point. Pour on to the egg yolk mixture in a thin stream, beating constantly and vigorously.
5 Put the pan over a moderate heat and cook, stirring constantly, until the mixture thickens. Add the lemon zest and juice and cook for a further 1-2 minutes until thick again. Pour the custard into a mixing bowl.
6 In a clean, dry bowl, whisk all 4 egg whites with the salt until standing in stiff peaks.
7 Add a little of the egg white mixture to the custard and mix lightly. Fold in the rest of the egg whites until well blended, then pour into the prepared soufflé dish.
8 Bake in the oven for 12-15 minutes until well puffed and golden. Serve the lemon soufflé at once.

in the egg yolks, whipped cream, crushed breadcrumbs and coffee and chicory essence.

5 Turn the mixture into a 1 L/2 pint metal container and cover securely with foil. Freeze for 2 hours, stirring lightly every 30 minutes, then leave for a further 2 hours, or until firm.

6 Let the ice cream stand at room temperature for about 5 minutes, to soften slightly.

7 Decorate ice cream with mint sprigs, if liked, and serve.

Lemon granita

SERVES 4-6

juice of 6 lemons

600 ml/1 pint water

175 g/6 oz sugar

lemon twists, to decorate

1 Put the water and sugar in a saucepan. Heat gently until the sugar has dissolved, then bring to the boil and boil for about 5 minutes, without stirring, until a thick uncoloured syrup is formed.

2 Remove the syrup from the heat and set aside until completely cold.

3 Add the lemon juice to the cold syrup and pour into a loaf tin or ice cube trays without the ice cube divisions. Freeze in the freezer compartment of a refrigerator or in the freezer for about 1 hour.

4 Remove from the freezer and stir well with a metal spoon until evenly blended.

5 Return to the freezer and freeze for a further 3 hours, stirring with a metal spoon once every 30 minutes during this time, to form an icy slush.

6 Spoon the granita into individual glass dishes, decorate with lemon twists and serve at once.

Brown bread ice cream

SERVES 4

50 g/2 oz fresh wholemeal breadcrumbs

25 g/1 oz sugar

2 large eggs, separated

50 g/2 oz light soft brown sugar, sifted, if lumpy

150 ml/¼ pint double cream, whipped until in soft peaks

1 tablespoon coffee and chicory essence, or dark rum

mint sprigs, to decorate (optional)

1 Heat the grill to high. Mix the breadcrumbs and sugar together; spread over the base of a small baking tray and toast under the grill for about 5 minutes, turning occasionally, until golden and crunchy.

2 Turn the crunchy crumbs on to a plate and leave to cool completely, then crush coarsely with the back of a wooden spoon.

3 Beat the egg yolks with a fork until well blended, then set aside.

4 In a spotlessly clean and dry large bowl, whisk egg whites until stiff. Whisk in brown sugar, 1 tablespoon at a time. Using a large metal spoon, fold

Melon glacé

SERVES 4

1 melon, weighing about 1 kg/2 lb

125 ml/4 fl oz water

50 g/2 oz sugar

225 ml/8 fl oz unsweetened white grape juice

2 tablespoons lemon juice

1 Pour the water into a heavy-based saucepan and add the sugar. Heat gently until the sugar has dissolved. Bring to the boil, without stirring, and boil for 1 minute. Leave the syrup to cool completely.

2 Cut the melon in half; remove and discard the seeds and any membrane. Scoop out all the flesh, drain and purée in a blender.

3 Measure out 600 ml/1 pint of the melon purée into a mixing bowl. Stir in the cold sugar syrup, grape juice and lemon juice. Spoon the mixture into a freezerproof container and cover with foil.

4 Freeze for 1-1½ hours until mushy around the edges. With a fork or wooden spoon, stir the mixture well. Cover and freeze for a further 1½-2 hours, stirring every 30 minutes. The ice is ready to serve when it has reached an evenly granular slushy consistency.

5 To serve: work the ice lightly with a fork then spoon into individual bowls set on ice.

Strawberry ice cream

SERVES 4

750 g/1½ lb strawberries, hulled
2 tablespoons frozen concentrated orange juice
225 ml/8 fl oz double cream
3 egg yolks
75 g/3 oz caster sugar
small sweet biscuits, to serve

1 Purée the strawberries in batches in a blender. Add the frozen orange juice to the strawberry purée and stir well to mix. Cover.

2 Pour the cream into a heavy-based saucepan, bring almost to the boil, then remove from the heat and leave to cool.

3 Whisk the egg yolks and sugar until pale and creamy then slowly stir in the cooled cream. Strain the mixture into a heatproof bowl.

4 Set the bowl over a pan half full of gently simmering water – check that the bottom of the bowl does not touch the water. Cook, stirring constantly until the custard is thick enough to thinly coat the back of the spoon. Remove the bowl from the pan, cover the custard closely with cling film and leave in a cool place until cold.

5 Stir the custard into the strawberry purée and pour the mixture into a freezerproof container. Cover and freeze for 1 hour, or until frozen about 1 cm/½ inch around the sides.

6 Turn the mixture into a bowl and whisk thoroughly to break up the ice crystals. Return to the container, cover and freeze for a further 1½-2 hours until firm.

7 Remove from the freezer and allow to soften for about 45 minutes in the refrigerator before serving.

8 To serve: scoop ice cream into individual glass dishes with an ice cream scoop and serve with crisp biscuits, if liked.

Yoghurt vanilla freeze

SERVES 4

2 eggs, separated
75 g/3 oz caster sugar
150 g/5 oz natural yoghurt
150 ml/¼ pint soured cream
1 teaspoon vanilla extract

Far left: Brown bread ice cream
Above: Strawberry ice cream

To serve

2-3 small oranges, peeled and cut into segments
2 kiwi fruit, peeled and sliced

1 Whisk together the egg yolks and sugar until pale and light. Then stir in the yoghurt, soured cream and vanilla extract and mix well.

2 Spoon the mixture into a freezerproof rigid container and place in the freezer for about 1½ hours until frozen solid around the edges but only softly frozen in the centre.

3 Whisk the egg whites until they stand in soft peaks, then fold them gently but thoroughly into the frozen mixture. Cover and return to the freezer for about 3 hours or until the mixture is solid.

4 Transfer to the main part of the refrigerator for 1 hour before serving, to allow the mixture to soften slightly.

5 To serve: scoop the vanilla freeze into the centre of 4 chilled small bowls, and surround with orange segments and kiwi slices.

Baked Fare

Who can resist the aroma of freshly baked bread or the
sight of a delectable sponge cake? Spoil yourself with any
of these sweet and savoury baked goodies.

Bara brith

MAKES 2 × 1KG/2 LB LOAVES

250 g/9 oz sultanas
125 g/4 oz currants
125 g/4 oz seedless raisins
500 g/1 lb light soft brown sugar
600 ml/1 pint warm strong tea, strained
1 egg, lightly beaten
750 g/1½ lb self-raising flour
2 teaspoons ground mixed spice
vegetable oil, for greasing
1 tablespoon clear honey, to glaze

1 Put the sultanas, currants, raisins and sugar in a bowl. Pour in the tea and stir well. Cover with a clean tea-towel and leave overnight.
2 Heat the oven to 170C/325F/Gas 3.
3 Grease and line with greaseproof paper two 1 kg/2 lb loaf tins. Grease the lining paper.
4 Stir the beaten egg well into the fruit and sugar mixture. Sift together the flour and spice, then stir into the mixture until thoroughly combined.
5 Divide the mixture equally between the prepared tins. Smooth the surface of each.
6 Bake the loaves in the oven for 1½ hours, then lower the heat to 140C/275F/Gas 1 and bake for a further 1½ hours, until a warmed fine skewer inserted into the loaves comes out clean.
7 Leave the loaves for a few minutes until cool enough to handle, then turn them out on to a wire rack. Invert the loaves the right way up.
8 Put the honey in a small saucepan and heat very gently. Brush the tops of the warm loaves with the heated honey, to glaze. Leave until completely cold before serving.

Marmalade cake

MAKES 8-10 SLICES

250 g/9 oz plain flour
1 teaspoon baking powder
½ teaspoon salt
½ teaspoon ground ginger
150 g/ 5 oz caster sugar
100 g/4 oz margarine or butter, diced
200 g/7 oz coarse cut orange marmalade
125 ml/4 fl oz milk
vegetable oil, for greasing

1 Heat the oven to 190C/375F/Gas 5. Lightly grease a loose-based 18 cm/7 inch square tin, line sides and base with greaseproof paper, then grease.
2 Sift the flour with the baking powder, salt and ginger into a bowl. Stir in the sugar. Add the margarine and rub it in with your fingertips until the mixture resembles even-sized breadcrumbs, then make a well in the centre of the mixture.
3 Add 50 g/2 oz marmalade and the milk and mix with a large metal spoon until thoroughly blended. Turn the mixture into the prepared tin and level the surface. Using a fork, gently spread the remaining marmalade over the top, to within 1 cm/½ inch of sides.
4 Bake the cake in the oven for 50-60 minutes, or until a warmed fine skewer inserted into the centre comes out clean. Cover the tin with greaseproof paper after 35 minutes baking to prevent the topping scorching.
5 Cool the cake for 5 minutes, then remove from the tin and carefully peel off the lining paper. Leave to cool completely on a wire rack. For a more mellow flavour, wrap in foil and store for 2-3 days before serving.

Banana teabread

MAKES 12 SLICES

225 g/8 oz self-raising flour
½ teaspoon ground mixed spice
100g/4 oz margarine
100 g/4 oz light soft brown sugar
2 eggs
500 g/1 lb soft bananas, mashed
1 tablespoon Demerara sugar
vegetable oil, for greasing

1 Heat the oven to 180C/350F/Gas 4. Grease a 1 kg/2 lb loaf tin, line the base with greaseproof paper, then grease the paper.
2 Sift the self-raising flour and mixed spice into a bowl.
3 Beat the margarine and sugar until pale and fluffy, then beat in 1 egg. Add the remaining egg and 1 tablespoon of the flour mixture and beat vigorously until evenly blended: a little flour prevents the mixture curdling when the second egg is added. Beat in the mashed bananas.
4 Using a large metal spoon, fold in the remaining flour mixture. Spoon the mixture into the prepared tin and level the surface, then sprinkle over the Demerara sugar.
5 Bake in the oven for 1-1¼ hours, or until firm to the touch.
6 Cool the teabread for 1 minute, then run a palette knife around the sides to loosen it, turn out of tin and peel off lining paper. Turn right way up and leave on a wire rack to cool completely before slicing. This teabread is moist enough to serve plain, but can be buttered, if liked.

Bara brith is good with cheese

Wholefood carrot cake

MAKES 12 SLICES

300 g/10 oz wholemeal flour
1 tablespoon baking powder
2 teaspoons ground mixed spice
100 g/4 oz shelled Brazil nuts, chopped
50 g/2 oz pressed dates, chopped
175 g/6 oz Muscovado sugar
125 ml/4 fl oz sunflower oil
125 ml/4 fl oz unsweetened apple juice
350 g/12 oz carrots, grated
sunflower oil, for greasing

To decorate

15 whole Brazil nuts
8 whole dried dates, halved and stoned
clear honey, to glaze

1 Heat the oven to 180C/350F/Gas 4. Grease a deep 18 cm/7 inch square cake tin. Line the sides and base with greaseproof paper, then thoroughly grease the lining paper.
2 Put the flour into a large bowl. Sift in the baking powder and spice and

Above: Spiced honey bars
Right: Cheese and walnut teabread

stir well to mix. Stir in the nuts and dates. Add the sugar, oil and apple juice and beat with a wooden spoon until blended. Stir in the carrots.
3 Turn the mixture into the prepared cake tin and level the surface. Arrange the nuts and halved dates in rows on top.
4 Bake in the oven for about 1¼ hours. (Cover with grease-proof paper after about 30 minutes baking to prevent overbrowning.)
5 Cool cake for 15 minutes, then turn out of tin and peel off lining paper. Place the cake, the right way up, on a wire rack and brush top with honey. Leave to cool before cutting.
● For a change, leave out the nut and date topping and decorate the cake with honey icing: mix 1 tablespoon clear honey into 75 g/3 oz icing sugar, then add enough water to give a thick pouring consistency. Spoon icing over cake, allowing it to run down the sides. Leave to set before cutting.

Spiced honey bars

MAKES 16 BARS

100 g/4 oz self-raising flour
1 teaspoon ground cinnamon
1 teaspoon ground mixed spice
1 teaspoon bicarbonate of soda
100 g/4 oz wholemeal flour
225 g/8 oz clear honey
juice and grated zest of 1 small orange
125 ml/4 fl oz vegetable oil
75 g/3 oz light soft brown sugar
2 eggs, well beaten
25 g/1 oz flaked almonds
melted margarine or vegetable oil, for greasing

1 Heat the oven to 180C/350F/Gas 4. Grease a 22 cm/8½ inch square cake tin, which is about 5 cm/ 2 inches deep. Line the base with greaseproof paper and then grease the paper.
2 Sift the self-raising flour with the ground spices and bicarbonate of soda into a large bowl. Stir in the wholemeal flour, then set aside.

3 Pour the honey into a large bowl. Measure the orange juice and make up to 150 ml/¼ pint with boiling water, then add to the honey and stir with a wooden spoon until blended. Stir in the oil, brown sugar, eggs and orange zest.

4 Pour the honey mixture on to the flour mixture and mix thoroughly to make a smooth batter. Pour the batter into the prepared tin and sprinkle the almonds over the top. Bake the cake in the oven for 50-55 minutes, until well risen and springy to the touch in the centre. (Cover with greaseproof paper after 40 minutes baking to prevent overbrowning.)

5 Cool the baked cake in the tin for 5 minutes, then run a palette knife around the edge, turn out on to a wire rack and peel off the lining paper — take care when turning out and removing the lining paper as the cake is very soft and cracks easily. Turn the cake the right way up. Leave to cool completely, then cut into 16 bars.

Cheese and walnut teabread

MAKES 8-10 SLICES

225 g/8 oz wholemeal flour
2 teaspoons baking powder
1 teaspoon celery salt
½ teaspoon mustard powder
50 g/2 oz margarine or butter, diced
100 g/4 oz Cheddar cheese, grated
25 g/1 oz shelled walnuts, chopped
150 ml/¼ pint milk
1 egg, beaten
vegetable oil, for greasing
butter, to serve

1 Heat the oven to 180C/350F/Gas 4. Grease a 500 g/1 lb loaf tin, line the base with greaseproof paper, then grease the paper.

2 Mix together the flour, baking powder, celery salt and mustard powder. Add the margarine and rub it in until the mixture resembles fine breadcrumbs. Stir in the cheese and walnuts, then mix in the milk and egg to make a soft dough.

3 Turn the dough into the prepared tin, level the surface and make a slight hollow in the centre. Bake for 40-45 minutes until the top of the loaf is golden brown and a warmed fine skewer inserted in the centre comes out clean.

4 Leave the loaf in the tin for a few minutes before turning it out on to a wire rack. Peel off the paper and leave right way up, to cool.

5 Serve the bread, thickly sliced and buttered.

Dundee cake

MAKES 10-12 SLICES

225 g/8 oz plain flour
1/4 teaspoon salt
50 g/2 oz ground almonds
100 g/4 oz currants
100 g/4 oz sultanas
100 g/4 oz seedless raisins
50 g/2 oz glacé cherries, rinsed, dried and
    chopped
50 g/2 oz chopped mixed peel
225 g/8 oz margarine or butter
225 g/8 oz light soft brown sugar
finely grated zest of 1 orange
finely grated zest of 1 lemon
4 eggs, lightly beaten
1 tablespoon sherry, brandy, orange juice or
    milk
40 g/1 1/2 oz whole blanched almonds
vegetable oil, for greasing

1 Heat the oven to 150C/300F/Gas 2. Grease a deep 20 cm/8 inch round cake tin, then line the base and sides with a double thickness of greaseproof paper. Lightly grease the paper with oil.
2 Sift the flour and salt into a bowl and stir in the ground almonds. In a separate bowl, mix the dried fruits, cherries and peel. Set aside.
3 Beat margarine, sugar and grated orange and lemon zest until pale and fluffy. Beat in the eggs, a little at a time, then fold in the sifted flour alternately with the fruit mixture. Stir in the sherry.
4 Spoon the cake mixture into the prepared tin, level the surface, then arrange the almonds on the top. Bake for about 3 hours until browned and firm to the touch. Cover the cake with greaseproof paper if it browns too fast but avoid opening the oven door for the first hour of cooking or the cake may sink.

5 Cool the cake for 30 minutes, then turn out of the tin and peel off the lining paper. Stand the cake the right way up on a wire rack and leave until cold.

Apricot spice scone

MAKES 8 SLICES

225 g/8 oz wholemeal flour
1 teaspoon bicarbonate of soda
1 teaspoon mixed spice
1/2 teaspoon ground ginger
1/2 teaspoon salt
50 g/2 oz butter, diced
100 g/4 oz dried apricots, chopped
150 g/5 oz natural yoghurt
vegetable oil, for greasing
plain flour, for dusting
butter, to serve
Topping
2 tablespoons milk
2 tablespoons Demerara sugar

1 Heat the oven to 220C/425F/Gas 7. Grease and flour a baking sheet.
2 Sift the flour, soda, spices and salt into a bowl. Tip the bran remaining in the sieve into the bowl. Add the butter and rub in until the mixture resembles fine breadcrumbs. Stir in the apricots. Add the yoghurt and mix until the dough is firm, then knead lightly until smooth.
3 Shape the dough into a round about 23 cm/9 inches across. Place on the baking sheet and mark into 8 wedges. Brush the top with the milk and sprinkle the sugar over.
4 Bake in the oven for 25 minutes. Transfer the scone to a wire rack to cool slightly and serve warm with plenty of butter.

Lemon dairy sponge

MAKES 6-8 SLICES

3 large eggs
75 g/3 oz caster sugar
75 g/3 oz plain flour
vegetable oil, for greasing
Filling and topping
150 ml/1/4 pint double cream
1 tablespoon milk
5 tablespoons lemon curd

1 Heat the oven to 190C/375F/Gas 5. Lightly grease two 18 cm/7 inch sandwich tins, line their bases with greaseproof paper, then lightly grease the paper.

2 Put the eggs and sugar into a heatproof bowl. Set the bowl over a pan of gently simmering water – check that the bottom of the bowl does not touch the water. Using a rotary or hand-held electric whisk, beat until the mixture is thick enough to hold the trail of the whisk for 3 seconds when the beaters are lifted.

3 Remove the bowl from the pan and whisk for a few minutes more, until the mixture is cool. Sift one-third of the flour over the mixture, then fold it in with a large metal spoon. Add the remaining flour in the same way, taking care not to over-mix.

4 Divide the mixture equally between the prepared tins and spread evenly by gently tilting the tins. Bake at once in the oven for 15 minutes, until the cakes are golden and springy to the touch.

5 Cool for 1-2 seconds, then turn out of the tins on to a wire rack. Peel off the lining paper and leave to cool completely.

6 To serve: whip the cream with the milk until standing in soft peaks. Place 1 cake on a serving plate and spread with half the lemon curd, then with half the cream. Place the other cake on top.

7 Put the remaining cream into a piping bag fitted with a small star nozzle. Spread the remaining lemon curd over the top of the cake. Pipe a border of cream around the top edge of the cake, then pipe a lattice over the lemon curd.

Gingerbread

MAKES 8-10 SLICES

225 g/8 oz plain flour
large pinch of salt
1½ teaspoons baking powder
½ teaspoon bicarbonate of soda
1 teaspoon ground ginger
½ teaspoon ground mixed spice
100 g/4 oz light soft brown sugar
75 g/3 oz margarine
75 g/3 oz black treacle
75 g/3 oz golden syrup
1 egg
125 ml/4 fl oz milk
grated zest of 1 orange
melted butter, for greasing

1 Heat the oven to 170C/325F/Gas 3. Lightly grease a deep 18 cm/7 inch square cake tin. Line the sides and base with greaseproof paper, then grease the lining paper.

2 Sift the flour with the salt, baking powder, bicarbonate of soda, ginger and mixed spice into a bowl.

3 Put the sugar, margarine, treacle and syrup in a heavy-based saucepan and stir over a low heat until the ingredients are melted and thoroughly blended. Remove from the heat and allow to cool slightly.

4 Beat the egg with the milk and pour on to the sifted flour mixture. Add the cooled melted treacle mixture and grated orange zest. Using a metal spoon, stir until thoroughly blended.

5 Pour the cake mixture into the prepared tin. Bake for about 1 hour, until the top of the gingerbread is firm to the touch.

6 Let the cake cool in the tin for 10 minutes before turning out on to a wire rack. Remove the lining paper and leave the cake to become quite cold. Wrap the cake in foil and store for 3 days before cutting.

---

*Far left: **Dundee cake***
*Below: **Lemon dairy sponge***

Frosted walnut cake

MAKES 6-8 SLICES

100 g/4 oz self-raising flour
pinch of salt
100 g/4 oz margarine or butter
100 g/4 oz caster sugar
2 eggs, beaten
50 g/2 oz walnuts, finely chopped
melted margarine or vegetable oil, for greasing
8 walnut halves, to decorate
Meringue frosting
175 g/6 oz caster sugar
pinch of salt
pinch of cream of tartar
2 tablespoons water
1 egg white
few drops of vanilla flavouring

1 Heat the oven to 180C/350F/Gas 4. Grease two 18 cm/7 inch sandwich tins. Line each base with greaseproof paper, then grease the paper.
2 Sift the flour and salt into a bowl and set aside. Beat the margarine and sugar together until pale and fluffy, then beat in the eggs, a little at a time. Fold in the sifted flour and chopped walnuts.

3 Divide the mixture equally between the prepared tins and level the surface. Bake the mixture in the oven, just above the centre, for about 25 minutes, until golden and springy to the touch.
4 Leave in the tins for 3 minutes, then turn out on to a wire rack and peel off the lining paper. Turn the cakes the right way up and leave to cool completely.
5 Make the meringue frosting: place the sugar, salt, cream of tartar, water and egg white in a heatproof bowl and beat together with a hand-held electric whisk for 30 seconds. Set the bowl over a pan of gently simmering water (check that the bottom of the bowl does not touch the water) and whisk at high speed for 5-7 minutes, until the frosting stands in peaks when the beaters are lifted out of the mixture. Remove the bowl of frosting from the pan of water and whisk in the vanilla flavouring.
6 Place 1 cake on a serving plate and spread with a little of the frosting. Put the remaining cake on top. Working quickly, pile the frosting on top of the cake and spread it over the top and sides with a palette knife, then mark it into decorative swirls.

7 Before the frosting sets, gently press the walnut halves around the top edge of the cake. Leave the frosting to set before serving.

Chocolate almond gâteau

MAKES 10-12 SLICES

100 g/4 oz plain flour
25 g/1 oz cocoa powder
4 eggs
175 g/6 oz caster sugar
vegetable oil, for greasing
Mocha filling
175 g/6 oz margarine or butter
350 g/12 oz icing sugar
4 teaspoons cocoa powder
4 teaspoons coffee and chicory essence
1 teaspoon dark rum
To decorate
100 g/4 oz apricot jam
1 tablespoon water
75 g/3 oz nibbed almonds
75 g/3 oz plain dessert chocolate, coarsely grated

1 Heat the oven to 190C/375F/Gas 5. Grease a deep 20 cm/8 inch round cake tin, then line the base with greaseproof paper and grease paper.
2 Sift the flour and cocoa powder into a bowl and set it aside.
3 Put the eggs and sugar into a large heatproof bowl. Set the bowl over a saucepan half-full of gently simmering water – check that the bottom of the bowl does not touch the water. Using a rotary whisk or hand-held electric whisk, beat until the mixture is thick enough to hold the trail of the whisk for about 3 seconds.
4 Remove the bowl from the pan and beat the mixture for a few minutes more until it is cool. Using a large metal spoon, fold in the sifted flour, one-third at a time.
5 Pour mixture into the prepared tin and spread evenly by gently tilting the tin. Bake immediately in the oven for 35-45 minutes until the surface is golden in colour and springy to the touch. Leave to stand in the tin for 1-2 seconds, then turn out on to a wire

Left: Serve Frosted walnut cake as a tea-time treat
Above right: Raspberry cream cake makes a great finale to a dinner party

rack. Peel off the lining paper and leave the cake to cool.

6 Meanwhile, make the filling: beat the margarine until creamy, then gradually beat in the icing sugar. Dissolve the cocoa in the coffee and chicory essence, then beat into the filling with the rum.

7 Heat the apricot jam with the water until runny, then pass through a sieve. Return to the pan and boil until it thickens to a coating consistency, then allow it to cool.

8 Using a long serrated knife, cut the cooled cake horizontally into three layers. Use half the filling to sandwich the layers together.

9 Brush the apricot jam around sides of cake, then press almonds on to the sides using a palette knife. Transfer to a serving plate.

10 Put the remaining filling in a piping bag fitted with a 1 cm/½ inch star nozzle and pipe a border around the top edge. Sprinkle the grated chocolate over the top of the cake, inside the border of cream.

Raspberry cream cake

MAKES 6-8 SLICES

100 g/4 oz self-raising flour

1 teaspoon baking powder

100 g/4 oz margarine

100 g/ 4 oz caster sugar

2 large eggs, beaten

1-2 drops vanilla extract

melted margarine, for greasing

icing sugar, to dredge

Filling

150 ml/¼ pint whipping cream

100 g/4 oz raspberries, defrosted if frozen

4-6 tablespoons raspberry jam

1 Heat the oven to 170C/325F/Gas 3. Grease the bases of two 18 cm/7 inch round sandwich tins and line them with greaseproof paper; grease the lining paper.

2 Sift the flour and baking powder into a large bowl. Add the margarine, caster sugar, eggs and vanilla extract and beat vigorously for 2-3 minutes until blended.

3 Divide the mixture equally between the prepared tins, level each surface and make a shallow hollow in the centre. Bake in the oven for 25 minutes until just firm to the touch.

4 Let the cakes stand in the tins for a few minutes before turning out on a rack (to prevent their delicate surface being marked place a tea-towel on the wire rack before turning out). Peel off lining paper. Turn cakes the right way up, then leave to cool completely.

5 Make the filling: whip the cream until stiff. Lightly crush the raspberries and fold them into the whipped cream.

6 Spread 1 cake with half the jam, then with the raspberry cream filling. Spread the underside of the other cake evenly with the remaining jam. Cut it into 6-8 wedges (cut a thin strip off the last wedge), then position these, jam-side down and slightly apart, on top of the filling. Sift icing sugar thickly over the top and serve.

Crispy lemon slices

MAKES 16 SLICES

75 g/3 oz margarine or butter
100 g/4 oz caster sugar
grated zest of 1 lemon
2 eggs separated
100 g/4 oz self-raising flour, sifted
150 g/5 oz natural yoghurt
40 g/1½ oz cut mixed peel
margarine, for greasing

Topping

100 g/4 oz caster sugar
juice of 1 small lemon

To decorate

16 crystallized mimosa balls
32 small diamonds of angelica

1 Heat the oven to 180C/350F/Gas 4. Grease a 28 × 18 cm/11 × 7 inch Swiss roll tin with margarine.
2 Beat the margarine, sugar and lemon zest together until pale and fluffy. Add the egg yolks, 1 at a time, beating thoroughly after each addition.
3 Using a large metal spoon, fold in the sifted flour alternately with the natural yoghurt. Fold in the peel.
4 Stiffly whisk the egg whites and fold them into the cake mixture, using a large, clean metal spoon to cut through the mixture.
5 Turn the mixture into the greased tin and spread it evenly. Bake in the oven for 15-20 minutes until the cake is a light golden colour and just firm to the touch.
6 Meanwhile, make the topping: mix together the caster sugar and lemon juice in a bowl to make a thin paste.
7 Allow the cake to stand in the tin for a few seconds, then carefully turn it out on to a wire rack and immediately spread the lemon paste over the surface. (The paste sinks in to make a crispy top.)
8 Leave the cake until quite cold before cutting into 16 rectangles with a sharp knife.
9 Just before serving, decorate the slices: arrange a crystallized mimosa ball and 2 diamonds of angelica on top of each slice.

Shortbread

MAKES 8 LARGE SLICES

150 g/5 oz butter at room temperature
75 g/3 oz caster sugar
200 g/7 oz plain flour
50 g/2 oz rice flour
caster sugar, to serve

1 Heat the oven to 170C/325F/Gas 3. Lightly grease and flour a 30 × 20 cm/12 × 8 inch Swiss roll tin or a 25 cm/10 inch flan tin with a loose base and fluted sides.
2 Beat the butter and sugar together until pale and fluffy. Sift both flours into the butter and sugar, then mix well to form a dough.
3 Press the dough evenly into the tin, levelling the surface, then prick the top of the shortbread all over. Bake in the oven for about 40 minutes, until golden brown.
4 Mark the shortbread into sections while hot, then leave it to cool in the tin before turning out.
5 Just before serving, sprinkle the shortbread with a little caster sugar. Break into sections to serve.

Oatcakes

MAKES ABOUT 24

250 g/9 oz fine or medium oatmeal
½ teaspoon baking powder
½ teaspoon salt
25 g/1 oz butter
3-4 tablespoons hot water
margarine, for greasing
fine or medium oatmeal, for sprinkling

1 Heat the oven to 200C/400F/Gas 6. Grease a baking sheet with margarine.
2 Put the oatmeal into a bowl with the baking powder, salt and butter. Mix together lightly with a fork, then add enough hot water to make a dough.
3 Sprinkle some oatmeal on a board and turn the dough on to this, kneading lightly. Roll out to a thickness of 3 mm/⅛ inch and cut into circles with a pastry cutter.
4 Transfer the oatcakes to the prepared baking sheet and bake for about 15 minutes, until firm.
5 Cool on the sheet for a few minutes, before transferring to a wire rack. Cool completely before serving.

Above left: Crisp and buttery Short bread is a Scottish favourite
Right: Almond-flavoured Macaroons are popular and elegant biscuits

Macaroons

MAKES 18

175 g/6 oz ground almonds

175 g/6 oz caster sugar

few drops of almond extract

few drops of vanilla extract

2 small egg whites, lightly beaten

blanched almonds, to decorate

caster sugar, for sprinkling

1 Heat the oven to 180C/350F/Gas 4. Line 2 large baking sheets with rice paper.

2 Put the ground almonds and caster sugar into a bowl and mix together well with a wooden spoon. Add the extracts, then gradually stir in just enough egg white to give a fairly stiff consistency.

3 Put the mixture into a piping bag fitted with a 1 cm/½ inch plain nozzle. Pipe nine 4 cm/1½ inch rounds on to each prepared baking sheet. Space rounds well apart, and away from the edges of the baking sheets, to allow room for spreading.

4 Place 1 almond in centre of each round; sprinkle lightly with caster sugar. Bake in the oven for 10-15 minutes, until just firm and beginning to colour.

5 Cool the biscuits for 1-2 minutes, then transfer to wire racks and leave to cool completely. Using your fingers, flake the excess rice paper off the biscuits. Serve at once, or store in a tin or other airtight container for up to 5 days.

High-fibre bread

MAKES 2 × 500 G/1 LB LOAVES

500 ml/18 fl oz warm water

1 tablespoon light soft brown sugar

1 tablespoon dried active yeast

550 g/20 oz wholemeal flour

125 g/4 oz bran

2 teaspoons salt

1 tablespoon sunflower oil

1 tablespoon kibbled wheat

sunflower oil, for greasing

1 Grease two 500 g/1 lb loaf tins.

2 Put 300 ml/½ pint water into a small bowl and stir in ½ teaspoon sugar and the yeast. Let stand for about 10 minutes, or until frothy.

3 Put the flour, bran, salt and remaining sugar into a large bowl and stir. Make a well in the centre and pour in the yeast mixture, the oil and 200 ml/7 fl oz water. Mix to a dough, then turn out on to a lightly floured surface and knead for 5 minutes.

4 Rinse out the mixing bowl, oil lightly and put in the dough. Cover with oiled polythene and leave in a warm place for 1 hour, until the dough has doubled in size.

5 Place the oven shelf in the centre of the oven and heat the oven to 230C/450F/Gas 8. Punch down the dough with your fist, then knead again for 1-2 minutes.

6 Divide the dough in half and shape each half into a loaf shape the length and width of the tins. Press the top of each loaf in kibbled wheat. Put the loaves into the tins, wheat side up, and press the dough down in corners.

7 Cover the loaves with oiled polythene and leave in a warm place for 20-30 minutes or until the dough has reached the top of tins.

8 Bake the loaves for 10 minutes, then reduce the heat to 200C/400F/Gas 6 and bake for a further 25 minutes, until the bread is crisp and brown and sounds hollow when removed from the tin and tapped on the base. Cool on a wire rack.

Rich corn bread

MAKES ABOUT 12 SLICES

100 g/4 oz cornmeal
100 g/4 oz self-raising flour
1 teaspoon bicarbonate of soda
50 g/2 oz caster sugar
2 eggs
150 ml/¼ pint milk
50 g/2 oz butter, melted
vegetable oil, for greasing

1 Heat the oven to 200C/400F/Gas 6. Grease a 20 cm/8 inch square baking tin.

2 Put the cornmeal in a large bowl, then sift the flour and bicarbonate of soda on top. Add the caster sugar and mix well.

3 Whisk the eggs with the milk, then gradually stir into the flour mixture to make a smooth batter. Add the melted butter and mix again.

4 Pour the batter into the prepared tin and level the surface. Bake for 25 minutes, until risen and golden brown. Cool the bread in the tin, then cut into squares to serve.

Cottage loaves

MAKES 8

500 g/1 lb strong white flour
1 teaspoon salt
1 teaspoon sugar
200 ml/7 fl oz warm water
1½ teaspoons dried active yeast
125 ml/4 fl oz warm milk
1 medium egg, beaten, to glaze
vegetable oil, for greasing

1 Sift the flour and salt into a bowl.

2 Dissolve the sugar in a little of the water. Sprinkle in the yeast and stir the mixture until smooth, then add the remaining water. Leave in a warm place until bubbles appear on the surface (3-5 minutes).

3 Make a well in the centre of the flour. Pour in the yeast mixture and the milk. Using a round-bladed knife, mix all the ingredients into a soft dough, adding a little extra warm water if necessary. Finish the mixing with your hands.

4 Knead the dough on a floured board for 5-10 minutes until it is

smooth and not sticky. Return it to the bowl and cut a cross on the top.

5 Cover the dough with a damp tea-towel or a sheet of greased polythene and leave in a warm place for about 1 hour, or until it has doubled in size.

6 Heat the oven to 200C/400F/Gas 6. Brush a large baking sheet with oil and dust it with flour.

7 Knead the dough again for 2-3 minutes. Divide the dough into 8 pieces. Cut each piece of dough into two unequal pieces. Shape into rounds. Place one small round on top of each large one. Push your finger through the centre of both, making sure that a hollow remains.

8 Place the shaped loaves on the prepared baking sheet and cover them loosely with a damp tea-towel or greased polythene. Leave them in a warm place for 10-20 minutes, until they have risen by about one-third.

9 Brush the loaves with beaten egg, avoiding the baking sheet, otherwise the loaves will stick to it.

10 Bake the loaves in the oven for approximately 20 minutes or until they are golden and sound hollow when tapped on base. Cool on wire racks.

Wheatmeal Chelsea buns

MAKES 8

125 ml/4 fl oz milk

1 egg, beaten

225 g/8 oz wheatmeal flour

½ teaspoon salt

25 g/1 oz butter, diced

25 g/1 oz light soft brown sugar

½ teaspoon ground mixed spice

7 g/¼ oz sachet easy-blend dried yeast

75 g/3 oz icing sugar

vegetable oil, for greasing

Filling

75 g/3 oz currants

25 g/1 oz cut mixed peel

50 g/2 oz light soft brown sugar

½ teaspoon ground mixed spice

50 g/2 oz butter, melted

1 Heat the milk in a pan until warm, then beat in the egg and set aside until required. Grease a 20 cm/8 inch sandwich cake tin.

2 Sift the flour and salt into a large bowl. Add the butter and rub in until the mixture resembles fine breadcrumbs. Stir in the sugar, spice and yeast, make a well in the centre and pour in the milk mixture. Using a fork, mix to a soft dough.

3 Turn the dough out on to a lightly floured surface and knead for about 10 minutes, until smooth.

4 Shape the dough into a ball and place in a large oiled bowl. Cover with oiled polythene and leave to rise in a warm place for 1-1½ hours or until doubled in size.

5 Meanwhile, make the filling: mix the currants with the peel, sugar and spice, then pour over the melted butter and stir well.

6 Turn out the risen dough on to a floured surface. Knead gently until the dough is back to original size, then roll into a 30 × 23 cm/12 × 9 inch rectangle. Pour filling over rectangle and spread to cover dough.

7 Starting at a short edge, roll up like a Swiss roll, to enclose the filling. Brush the end with water and press firmly to seal, then slice across into 8 pieces.

8 Place 1 piece, cut-side up, in the centre of the prepared tin. Arrange the remaining pieces around it so that they are just touching. Cover with oiled polythene and leave in a warm place for 45 minutes or until risen.

9 Heat the oven to 200C/400F/Gas 6.

10 Bake the buns in the oven for about 30 minutes until risen and golden brown. Transfer to a wire rack and leave to cool completely.

11 Make the icing: sift the icing sugar into a bowl, then stir in enough water to give a smooth coating consistency. Drizzle the icing over the top of the cooled buns before serving.

Flowerpot loaf

MAKES 8-10 SLICES

175 g/6 oz strong white flour

175 g/6 oz strong wholemeal flour

1 teaspoon salt

15 g/½ oz margarine, diced

1 teaspoon easy-blend dried yeast

200 ml/7 fl oz hand-hot water

1 tablespoon bulgur wheat

milk, to glaze

vegetable oil, for greasing

1 Season an unused, clean earthenware flowerpot measuring 13 cm/5½ inches across the top and 12 cm/5 inches tall: to prevent the loaf from sticking, brush the inside of the pot very thoroughly with oil, then place the empty pot in a 200C/400F/Gas 6 oven for 15 minutes. Allow to cool.

2 Mix the flours together in a large bowl with the salt. Rub in the fat, then sprinkle in the yeast and stir well to mix. Pour in the water and mix to a firm dough.

3 Turn the dough out on to a floured surface and knead for 10 minutes, or until it is smooth and elastic, then shape it into a round.

4 Brush the inside of the seasoned pot very thoroughly with oil, then sprinkle in 2 teaspoons bulgur.

5 Place the dough in the prepared pot, pressing it down well. Cover with oiled polythene and leave in a warm place for about 1¼ hours, or until the dough has risen just above the pot.

6 About 20 minutes before the dough is risen, heat the oven to 230C/450F/Gas 8.

7 Uncover the dough and brush the top with milk. Sprinkle over the remaining bulgur and press it down lightly. Bake loaf in the oven for 30-35 minutes, until the top of the loaf is browned and crusty.

8 Cool the loaf for 2-3 minutes, then run a palette knife around the sides to loosen it. Turn the loaf out of the pot, then place the right way up on a wire rack and leave to cool completely before cutting into slices.

Above left: Cottage loaves
Below: Flowerpot loaf

Orange iced buns

MAKES 8

280 g/10 oz packet white bread mix
finely grated zest of 1 large orange
25 g/1 oz caster sugar
200 ml/7 fl oz hand-hot water
plain flour, for dusting
vegetable oil, for greasing
To decorate
175-200 g/6-7 oz icing sugar
4½ teaspoons strained freshly-squeezed
*   orange juice*
few drops of orange food colouring
crystallized orange slices (optional)

1 Grease a large baking sheet with vegetable oil.
2 Put the bread mix into a bowl, then stir in the orange zest and caster sugar. Mix thoroughly. Add the water and mix well, first with a wooden spoon and then with your hand to make a firm dough.
3 Turn the dough out on to a lightly floured surface and knead for 5 minutes, then divide into 8 equal pieces. Shape each piece into a round, then roll each round to an oval, about 10 cm/4 inches long.
4 Transfer the oval buns to the prepared sheet, spacing them well apart. Cover with oiled polythene and leave in a warm place for about 1 hour, or until the oval buns are risen and have doubled in bulk.
5 About 20 minutes before the buns are risen, heat the oven to 220C/425F/Gas 7.
6 Uncover the buns and bake in the oven for 15 minutes, or until they are golden brown and sound hollow when tapped with your knuckles on the base. Transfer the buns to a wire rack and leave to cool completely.
7 Make the icing for decoration: sift 175 g/6 oz icing sugar into a bowl, then stir in the orange juice. The icing should be thick enough to coat the buns: if it is too runny, stir in a little more sifted icing sugar. Tint the icing very pale orange with a few drops of food colouring.
8 Spread a little icing over the top of each bun. Decorate with crystallized orange slices, if liked, then leave the buns for about 30 minutes or until the orange icing is firm and set.
9 The buns are best served fresh on the day of making.

Lusciously-filled Devon scones

Devon scones

MAKES 7-8

225 g/8 oz plain flour
1 teaspoon cream of tartar
½ teaspoon bicarbonate of soda
½ teaspoon salt
50 g/2 oz margarine or butter, diced
125-150 ml/4-5 fl oz milk
vegetable oil, for greasing
plain flour, for dusting
To serve
3-4 tablespoons strawberry jam
125 g/4 oz clotted or double cream

1 Heat the oven to 230C/450F/Gas 8. Grease and lightly flour a large baking sheet.
2 Sift the flour with the cream of tartar, bicarbonate of soda and salt, then sift again into a large bowl. Add the diced margarine and rub it in until the mixture resembles fine bread-crumbs. Make a well in the centre.

3 Pour in most of the milk and mix to a soft (but not sticky) dough with a fork, adding a little more of the milk if necessary. Gather the dough into a ball, turn it out on to a lightly floured surface and knead it lightly and briefly until smooth. The dough should be mixed quickly and handled as lightly as possible, otherwise the scones will be tough and heavy.
4 Either pat or lightly roll out the dough to a round about 1 cm/½ inch thick. Using a 7.5 cm/2½ inch round pastry cutter, cut out as many scones as possible. Lightly knead the trimmings together, pat or roll out again and cut out more scones.
5 Brush the tops of the scones with milk and place on the prepared baking sheet. Bake in the oven, just above the centre, for about 15 minutes until risen and browned. Wrap the scones in a clean tea-towel and leave to cool.
6 Scones do not keep well and should be served fresh on the day of making.
7 To serve: split each scone in half with your fingers, spread the bottom half with jam and the top with clotted cream, then lightly replace the top half of the scone.

Index